ChapWoman's Almanac Two

ChapWoman's Almanac

Pilot Handling Throughout the Year

ANNE LORIMER SIRNA
ILLUSTRATIONS BY SAM NICHOLS

Seven Seas Press
Camden, Maine

Published by Seven Seas Press/International Marine Publishing
Company

10 9 8 7 6 5 4 3 2 1

Library of Congress Cataloging-in-Publication Data

Sirna, Ann Lorimer.
    ChapWoman's alwomanac / Ann Lorimer Sirna.
        p.   cm.
    ISBN 0-915160-98-6
    1. Sailing—Humor.   I. Title.
PN6231.S15S57   1989
818'.5402—dc20   89-15326
                                                          CIP

International Marine Publishing Company offers software for sale.
For information and a catalog, please contact TAB Software
Department, Blue Ridge Summit, PA 17294-0850.

Questions regarding the content of this book should be addressed to:

Seven Seas Press/International Marine Publishing Company
Division of TAB Books, Inc.
P.O. Box 220
Camden, Maine 04843

Typeset by Camden Type 'n Graphics
Printed by Edwards Brothers, Lillington, NC
Illustrated by Sam Nichols
Production by Janet Robbins
Edited by Cynthia Bourgeault

edication

To Graeme Lorimer
my father, my teacher, my friend

ontents

Preface

Ahoy Again Fellow Mates,

We're back on board with a new ChapWoman's Guide—*ChapWoman's Al(wo)manac*.

We wish we could raft up with each of you, swap sea stories and watch the sun set and the moon rise topside. Since we can't, we hope our book will cruise with you in our place.

You have written to us from the Caribbean, Puget Sound, the Chesapeake Bay, Canada, Maine, and every bay and river in between. Some of you are liveaboards, some are cruisers, and others are reluctant Saturday sailors, but all your captains sound just like ours. In fact, many of you thought we had been sailing with *your* man of the sea! You told us that *Chap-Woman's Guide to Shemanship and Pilot Handling* told it like it is but didn't tell it all.

So come sailing with us aboard *Mischief* each month of the year in *ChapWoman's Al(wo)manac*.

Listen to the symphony of sailing—the swoosh of the breeze filling the sails, the grind and squeak of the winches, the slap of waves against hull, the mournful cry of the bell buoy guarding the rocks, and the thunk of lines on the deck.

There's a dog named Howlyard and passengers like Walt and Daisy. Walt wants a "water experience" and runs the boat aground instead. Daisy wants to stay home.

You'll join *Mischief's* crew bareboating in the Grenadines in February, racing in June, cruising to Block Island in July, and buying a new boat in November. Perhaps your captain, like ours, has been lusting after an integrated instrument system. Electronics are to a man what upholstery is to a woman.

Once again we've written *ChapWoman's* for the woman afloat. She is the one who must keep smiling while handling both the winch and the customer's son, who is trying to unscrew the through-hull fittings; she is the only one who will agree to accompany the captain to the "do-it-yourself" yard in March, before the head is working; and she is the one who is startled to discover that a lifetime of good manners can vanish in a single afternoon of racing.

But let's face it—we women of the sea are resourceful. It doesn't take us long to persuade the captain that boating with customers may be good for business but bad for the boat, or to discover that on race day a bellowed "steel hull" wins more respect than "starboard tack." And we feel a bit smug when we are ready for launch before our marina mates have begun to sand their boats' bottoms.

We have included an astrological guide to your captain. Stubborn Taurus is never off course. It is the Baltimore light that has moved. Life-of-the-party Sagittarius has his nettle pool shut down by the marine police. Cancer is into doom and gloom. His will be the craft that vanishes in the Bermuda Triangle. When precise Virgo sets anchor his hand signals look more like the Super Bowl than instructions to the helm.

We've written *ChapWoman's* for you, so rendezvous with us—and bring your friends along too.

Anchors Aweigh,

Anne Lorimer Sirna

Anne Lorimer Sirna

ChapTWOoman's Al₁ᵂᴼmanac

January

In January your captain is a miserable man. He has swallowed the anchor and retired to the basement, which he now calls a sail loft. *Mischief* is up on blocks. There he sits, mournfully waiting for spring, buttressed by boat cushions and sail bags. His toy has been taken away from him by that big bully Winter.

He reads marine catalogs by the light of the ship's lantern, orders bottom paint, and dreams of an early commissioning. He makes more teak shelves and racks than *Mischief* can hold; teak oil is his kind of aphrodisiac. For recreation he reads *The 12-Volt Doctor's Alternator Book*. Howlyard the sea dog curls up on the life jackets and waits for a better time.

So do you. You worry about money for Uncle Sam and he worries about money to pay the marina. Sure, Uncle Sam may send you to jail, but what's a little jail compared to "No cash no splash," he says. It's important to keep your priorities straight.

You're tired of getting seasick in his car while he listens to his tape of "Sailboat." The surf crashes, the boat creaks, buoys clang, gulls cry, and he grips his spoked steering wheel and leers like a lunatic. You wonder if he's been around the piling once too often.

He becomes a lecture groupie, sloshing through snowdrifts in seaboots and sou'wester, oiled wool sweater and Greek fisherman's cap to see slides of the Intracoastal. Perhaps he seems a wee bit out of place among the navy blazers, but at least he's beaming at the blue water, white sails, and luscious ladies lounging about in shorts. He grins foolishly at a nubile miss handling the jib while his friend Sam pokes him in the ribs.

"Isn't she a beaut!" he chortles.

"Sure is. Saw her in Annapolis last summer," your captain says while you stiffen and listen up and try to remember where you have seen that blonde before. You relax when he says that her Barient winches are better than your Lewmars. For just an instant you forgot the old sailing maxim: When a sailor looks at a pretty girl on a boat he sees the boat.

It's important to keep your priorities straight.

It is still January when you notice a light in your captain's eye, a lilt in his voice, and a lift in his step. Why? Because the New York Boat Show is looming on the horizon.

"Let's spend a day in New York," he says. The Jacob K. Javits Center has never been your favorite port of call in the Big Apple. Broadway and Bergdorf's, the Whitney, and tea at the Plaza are more to your liking.

You suggest a matinee first or a quick trip to the Metropolitan, but no, he wants to go right to the show. He might miss something—although you can't imagine what, since boats without sails, indoors, in January aren't going anywhere.

You do agree that you are just browsing, not buying. Particularly since there is only $.67 in your account until Friday. Last year you bought the Loran and the year before the cockpit cushions, but this year *Mischief* has everything she needs. Your captain says that all he wants is to take a break from winter.

Usually he does not suffer waiting in line gladly, but today he stands patiently for 30 minutes to buy his ticket. He's deep in conversation with Oscar from the Bronx.

Oscar wants to spend his tax refund on a 19-footer with a porta potty. Your captain suggests a head, and before you

2

know it he's off on the merits of Sea Lube and the drama of unclogging the head in the middle of the ocean. Oscar is hanging on his words. His wife looks sick. She does not join in the conversation. Under ordinary circumstances, your one and only does not talk toilets with strangers, but today is different. ChapWoman has noticed that there are no strangers at boat shows—only fellow sailors you have yet to meet.

Once inside, your captain is a salesman's dream. He talks as if he is definitely going to buy and the sky's the limit.

Last year it was diesels. This year he is into refrigeration. He spends a lot of time talking earnestly to an eager salesman about the length of time it takes to make an ice cube. This is a man who has never refilled an ice tray in his life. The salesman says 45 minutes from water to ice. Frankly, it has never occurred to you to stand watch while water turns hard in a little plastic tray.

After debating the ice cube in depth, he cruises over to the lazyjacks and Stack-Packs and self-furling mains. He asks the salesman what's new in fully battened mains. He says he's going to Nova Scotia for the summer. You stand slack-jawed. Nova Scotia is news to you.

You relax when you remember that you don't have a fully battened main and that your captain is in charge of your annual sailing club cruise to Williamsburg. No wonder you feel a little giddy and lightheaded at boat shows. It's not climbing all those ladders; it's the amount of hot air being exchanged around you.

For a second you forgot that your captain has no intention of buying anything. Boat show talk is his kind of therapy. Where else could he find so many people paid by somebody else to listen to him talk about his dreams and fantasies? A psychiatrist would cost $100 an hour. Come to think of it, what harm would it do to try a little therapy yourself?

"What about a spinnaker?" you inquire brightly. Why not? Compared to ice cubes and Stack-Packs, this could be fun—a little like shopping for a prom dress for *Mischief*. It's always sort of bothered you how her old red, white, and blue spinnaker clashes with her green hull. Besides, you're only looking.

ChapWoman cautions that this is a very dangerous move. In the midst of boat show euphoria, two may do together what one would never consider alone.

It stretches into the dining room and on down the hall.

Immediately the salesman turns his tanned, terrific countenance in your direction and smiles dazzlingly. You are given the decided feeling that he's been waiting all his life to unburden his soul to you in an impassioned discourse on the merits of cruising versus racing spinnakers. He offers to follow this outpouring with a brief slide show. Moved by his fervor, you acquiesce. You haven't any money, but it's kind of fun to be so involved in a discussion about sailing.

Next, the salesman (whose name naturally is Biff) whips out his collection of spinnaker silks. You remember the billowing spinnakers on the bay last summer, the warm breeze, the perfect day. Biff says that it is important that you pick your colors, design your sail. Biff says that a spinnaker is an individual statement. It tells the world who you are.

Perhaps the green, purple, and white, you muse. Purple is in this year, and *Mischief* would look stunning in that combination. Or perhaps even green, purple, and turquoise. . . .

"We're thinking of red, orange, yellow, and black," the captain says.

"Oh no, not those hot colors," you blurt. "It's got to be cool pastels—to go with the hull."

You see the spinnaker and smile.

The captain agrees with you that green would look good but is definitely resistant to purple. He proposes green, yellow, and black. No black you say. "Well what if we put all our colors together to make a rainbow?" "Aye Aye," you say and before you know it, young Biff is grinning broadly as he writes on his pad and tells you the delivery date and that of course they take plastic. No need to worry about anything as crass as money now.

Driving home you remind each other that you weren't going to buy anything at the boat show, that the Christmas bills are still on the desk, and that the mortgage is due.

When your spinnaker finally arrives you spread it out on the living room floor. It stretches into the dining room and on down the hall. Soon the whole downstairs is clothed in your rainbow spinnaker. It is a glorious sight. You put Howlyard in the garage and the kids in the kitchen while you figure out how to pack it. Even on the floor it has a life of its own.

Good old Biff has included a few scraps of extra material in the package so the captain ties a bit of spinnaker to the car

5

aerial. Toting your groceries through slush and sleet, you see the spinnaker floating wild and free from your car and you smile. Sailing season isn't that far away.

February

At first you think you are dreaming when the captain suggests a Caribbean cruise. Visions of sunshine, bouillon on deck, sumptuous meals and being pampered—particularly that—dance round your head. It is too good to be true.

You're right. He plans a bareboat charter with his sailing buddies Matt and Paul. No sunning on the deck with a book in Virgin Gorda or exploring the caves at Norman Island for you. You're going to the Grenadines, where 25-knot tradewinds never stop blowing, boats sail on their sides, and the crew clutches the rail like the twisted divi-divi trees clinging to the shore. It's bluewater survival, not sedentary pursuits. When the United States fleet visited the Grenadines it was for a war.

Your first impulse is to stay home or hold out for a cruise ship to Saint Thomas or bareboating in the Virgins where you won't have to stand on one leg for a week. But after talking to Pat and Alice, the other mates, you change your mind. With three captains on deck there won't be anything for the mates to do topside and since you have agreed to hold out for split provisioning there won't be much below. Forget about the pampering—you'll settle for the sunshine and sumptuous meals out.

But which of the three men will be *The Captain?*

"Matt," says your one and only. "Paul and I are going to relax, crew, and enjoy ourselves." After long years of service you know that there is no joy in being crew, but why burst his bubble?

"Matt can worry about sail trim and the anchor dragging at three a.m. We'll do as we are told."

You laugh rudely. Not to be a spoilsport, but your captain has never done as he was told or taken orders, particularly from Matt, whom he considers the new boy on the dock. He is not a team player. He is Attila the Hun.

So that night you lie in bed wrestling with the nitty-gritty. Can three captains who have been friends for 20 years, and who all own their own boats, sail happily ever after in the

Grenadines without mutiny, mayhem, or murder? The answer is no.

Particularly because your captain is analytical, Paul is laid-back, and Matt is fussy. Matt motors a lot and Paul never breaks out the iron jib. Your captain studies wind and weather, currents and charts before he sets sail. Paul just goes where the wind blows and Matt hangs out in the slip. Your captain reefs too much too soon and Paul gets knocked down because he never reefs at all. They don't even cleat lines the same way. The awful truth is that you are going to lose your summer rafting mates.

Disaster may lie ahead but your arrival on a mountaintop in Saint Vincent is jovial—in spite of the fact that it reminds Paul of catching a carrier hook. You are playing hooky from winter. While the hot island sun relaxes your body and warms your soul, the crystal clear blue-green water and pure white sand beaches delight your spirit. The captains are clapping each other on the back and agreeing that there is nothing like a Caribbean vacation with old friends.

Your worries from home seem silly, but the charter company gives you some new ones. Their litany of don'ts throws a pall over the holiday and makes you think that you are about to star in *Jaws:*

> Don't swim at night because of sharks.
> Don't wear jewelry in the water because the glitter will attract sharks.
> Don't go in the water with an open cut because your blood will attract sharks.
> Don't sail at night because the reefs will gouge your boat, and you will sink and attract sharks.

"Don't sail at all. Go to a hotel," says Alice.

But when you see your 42-foot charter boat *Merrily* straining at her docklines, the sharks are forgotten and you are eager to set sail—too eager perhaps, since Matt and Paul override your captain's desire to check out systems.

"We've paid for it to be in good shape. Let's go," says Paul.

"You never get what you pay for," says your captain ominously.

Each captain strides purposefully to the helm. It's a wee bit crowded back there. Yours and Paul grin sheepishly.

"Forgot who was captain," says Paul, laying the halyard line loosely around the cleat.

"Belay that line," orders Matt. Paul frowns, then gives a mock salute.

"Right on, Bligh."

The mates nod knowingly. ChapWoman would suggest that if two women in the kitchen is the Chinese sign for trouble, then three captains on a boat are anybody's disaster.

At first all goes well. The men cast off, *Merrily* heels over on a starboard tack, and the mates sing "Row, Row, Row Your Boat" and agree that February in the sun is a dream. The treacherous coral reefs look as innocent as white lace chocolate candy. Sun and wind lull you into complacency by the time Matt decides to drop anchor in a cove for lunch.

One of Matt's problems is that he can't make up his mind. He motors around and around in circles trying to find the right piece of water. Paul, who is known to sail in and drop anchor in 30 seconds, is exasperated. Your captain bellows suggestions from the bow. Paul, holding the anchor, keeps shouting, "For God's sake, let's drop it." Matt motors on mesmerized.

Finally he gives the signal and down goes the plow. He heads up and issues instructions about dropping the second anchor. Your captain is methodically stretching anchor chain and rode along the side of the deck the way he does in the bay. Paul says it's a waste of time. Matt is bawling over the wind and giving hand signals. Paul, still exasperated, gives a hand signal that has nothing to do with boating. You're not sure whether they planned to drop the anchor when they did or whether in the confusion of rode, chain and hand signals they kicked it over by mistake, but it really doesn't matter. It wasn't cleated to *Merrily*. Anchor, chain, and rode sink to the bottom. The atmosphere topside is far from merry.

Matt shouts some more.

"Always cleat your ground tackle before laying it out," admonishes Paul.

"That was your job," barks your captain. You wonder if Paul knows that your captain never makes a mistake. Other people make them.

Paul and your captain dive and dive for the anchor, which is much farther down than it looks. They are running out of

Your long-anticipated luxury cruise is a bareboat charter. You cook squid.

breath and patience when Matt refers to them as a couple of landlubbing wimps who don't know how to cleat an anchor. It's a joke but nobody laughs. Your captain fixes Matt with an icy stare. He has never been called a wimp before.

Luckily at this tense moment an eleven-year-old girl from a neighboring boat splashes over and offers to help. Down she goes and up comes the anchor.

"Ouch," howls Matt as Pat kicks him in the shins before he mentions wimp again. Sensitivity has never been his long suit.

It is now that you recall the exact words of the charter brochure. "Bareboat cruising can be sheer magic for the right people. What could be better than congenial friends sailing together against the backdrop of the Caribbean?" At this precise moment you can think of a lot of things that could be better, so you and Pat and Alice jump ship the minute you arrive in Bequia, leaving the captains to silently coil and cleat their lines.

The boat may not be magic but certainly Bequia is. Palms, bougainvillea, hibiscus, and camelias cluster about thatched-roofed, windowless houses. Before meeting the captains in the hotel bar you buy big straw hats and bunches of bananas to ripen on the boom. A cocktail hour of rum punches and sea stories with other mariners has smoothed over the wounds of the afternoon. They delight in telling you that the bar stools are made of whale scrotum, which is one of those facts you'd rather not know. Perhaps tomorrow will be a better day.

It won't. You awaken to discover the lettuce and tomatoes are frozen into ice balls and the engine won't start.

"We should have checked systems," intones your captain as they remove the companionway steps and elbow each other out of the way. All three peer at the monster lying silently below. They argue about why it won't start, what to do to make it start, and which parts to remove first. If it blows up they'll all go together. The discussion and disagreement continues until they give up, shoot it with ether, and off you go.

Alice chooses this moment to hit the head to wash her hair, and the automatic pressure switch on the pump chooses this moment to fail. A call to the charter company brings the good news that a new pump will be waiting at Union Island. The bad news is that Union Island is several days away. And as Alice reminds anybody who will listen, she is already lathered with soap.

"We should have checked systems before we left," mutters your captain. A Greek chorus has nothing on him.

"No problem. We'll bypass the power to the pump and turn it on and off by hand," says Paul.

"No way," says Matt. "That switch is a safety. Without it we could run down the batteries or have a fire."

Alice, who is in the shower covered with soap, couldn't care less about batteries or fire. At last they decide to bypass to get Alice out, but Matt is not happy about it.

"See what happens when you neglect systems?" says your captain.

Your next port of call is Mustique, where you will have dinner ashore at the Cotton House Club. But first you must dock the Mediterranean way. ChapWoman warns that Mediterranean mooring is not for the faint of heart. You must maneuver backwards into your slip while the wind is blowing. There are no finger piers or cheater lines to guide you and naturally your boat does not back to port. All you have are two gleaming, very expensive hulls on either side and the prospect of a lawsuit if you hit either one.

The smoothness of your docking varies inversely with the number of people standing on the dock.

The procedure goes like this: Find an empty slip (often the hardest step) and swoop down upon it, doing your best to scare off all other pretenders; round up just before you crash into the slip nose first and then drop your bow anchor; back in without hitting port or starboard vessel; catch the two back pilings and make fast to them, which is not easy unless a member of the crew has eight-foot arms; do all this under the watchful gaze of everybody in the marina.

Oh yes, there are many mariners on their boats. Back home where boating manners count they would leap to your assistance, cleating lines and offering a "well done."

But here in Mustique, where the Beautiful People hobnob with Princess Margaret and the Royalty on million-dollar yachts, they do not speak to charterers. They laugh at them. Charterers, like the early Christians, provide the afternoon's entertainment. Yachtsmen settle into their cockpits with cool, frosty drinks, eagerly awaiting the afternoon sport.

You do not disappoint them. Matt is at the helm. On the first try it is obvious that he has misjudged and is going to ride up the transom of the very expensive vessel to port. Out he goes to try again. This time the wind blows the bow off and he misses the slip entirely. He tries making a big circle that will allow him to back to starboard and still make the slip. He is turning red-faced with frustration or humiliation—you aren't sure which. He tries again and again. ChapWoman would mention the boating maxim that the number of people watching varies inversely with the ease of your docking. Right now Matt is playing to standing room only.

"Damn tub won't back to port. We'll have to anchor out unless one of you hotshot skippers wants to try."

Obviously your captain takes the helm. At first he doesn't fare any better than Matt, but after analyzing the wind and the current and the size of the arc needed to back into the slip with a boat that doesn't back to port, he succeeds in starting into the slip without hitting port or starboard boat. Matt and Paul prepare to catch the pilings; your captain preens a bit as he nears the bulkhead.

Matt and Paul go as far as to say "good job," when suddenly in the midst of all this male bonding and self-congratulation Alice screams, "Look out," and the audience on all sides bursts out laughing. This is what they came for. Your captain has forgotten that there is a dinghy on the stern of the boat he has just succeeded in backing successfully to port.

Not an inexpensive little dinghy but a great big pricey Boston Whaler with an equally pricey engine on the back worth thousands and thousands of dollars. What is about to happen is too awful to watch but you watch anyway. First the dinghy is tucked against *Merrily's* stern, then it crunches, and then it sinks engine and all. There it lies in full view in the crystal clear water, soaking up the blue Caribbean Sea.

The three men speak in measured tones since the delighted dockside crowd is straining to hear who says what to whom. Matt says the captain should remember he is towing a dinghy. Your captain says he had enough to do getting into a slip—a slip that another captain he knows couldn't get into; Paul says he was busy tying up.

Pat, who teaches second graders, speaks in her best firm but soothing voice. "I think we can all work together to raise the dinghy."

"Why not winch it up on the main halyard?" you say.

The captains ignore you. They stand silently staring at the drowned dinghy. After a few minutes your captain speaks.

"One of us can winch it up using the main halyard while the others can tip the water out as it raises."

"Good idea," says Matt.

"Let's get at it," says Paul enthusiastically.

You are filled with righteous indignation—it was your idea.

Pat raises her finger to her lips. "Shhhh." She understands playground dynamics.

Now that they have a common cause the captains work shoulder to shoulder to raise the dinghy, remove the engine, and race it to shore like a transplant organ. Luckily there is a repair shop a block away where the owner flushes it out, and gets it running. It is one of hundreds of charter boat engines that has come his way. The dinghy has a few new nicks and dings, but other than you seem to be home free—at least till you get back to the charter company.

The next day you do not stop for lunch or a swim but sail on your side for five hours to reach Union Island in time to pick up the new pump. The wind drowns out conversation. It would be quite easy to go mad in a wind that never stops blowing by day and rattles the rigging by night.

The charter company neglected to warn you that the harbor at Union Island has no good holding ground. Every time Matt drops the anchor it drags. Finally after one hour and 17 tries it holds, but no sooner are you in place than a topless lady captain with a long braid hanging down her back pulls up alongside you. The men hasten to the rail.

"Captain," she says in a heavy French accent. All three captains leap to attention. "Please, my anchor it no hold. Please shorten line," she smiles and the captains grin foolishly.

Just in case he's a little distracted, which you know he is, you remind your captain in no uncertain terms that it took one hour and 17 tries to find any holding ground. If you shorten line you will drag.

"What's a little rode among friends?" says Paul, full of largesse.

"A lot," says Alice in a voice that means business. The war between the sexes is in full tilt aboard *Merrily*.

Reluctantly Matt tells his mermaid that he is not going to shorten rode, at which point she yells so many obscenities at you in French that you don't need a dictionary to understand what she is saying.

"Too bad you gals don't have any boating esprit de corps. Now we can't have her over for drinks," lament the captains as you dinghy in to dinner.

When you return, *Merrily* is gone. The Frenchwoman's boat is anchored and holding fast.

"That's impossible. That anchor held for three hours," says your captain.

"Unless somebody got on board and pulled up the rode," you say darkly.

"Hell hath no fury like a woman scorned," chimes Alice.

Pat, who is always practical, suggests that the first order of business is to find the boat since it will be difficult to explain to the charter company that not only did you sink their dinghy but also lost their boat.

So you all clamber aboard the dinghy with flashlights in search of *Merrily*. Your flashlights are not a welcome addition to the peaceful anchorage where romantic couples are enjoying the balmy Caribbean night topside.

At last you see *Merrily* peacefully drifting toward a white sand beach. Fortunately for you and the charter company she has not arrived.

"We have to anchor again," groans Pat.

"This could take all night,"chimes Alice.

"I've got a better idea," says the captain. "How 'bout rafting up with the Frenchwoman?"

March

Outside your window there's one solitary robin pecking through last week's snow. Foolish bird. It looks like winter, it feels like winter, and Mr. Red Breast is thinking nest building.

He's not alone. Your captain checks the calendar like the Supreme Commander preparing for the Normandy Invasion. Spring is only two weeks away. He is humming. That's a bad sign. You worry when he hums, particularly when the tune is "What Do You Do with a Drunken Sailor?" and it is still cold and still March.

He strides purposefully through the basement collecting ladders and surgical masks, extension cords and sander, grinder, bottom paint, and rubbing compound. You scurry about searching for rags. Perhaps some of the kids' T-shirts—they look like rags anyway.

It is D-Day, H-Hour. Time to attack the boatyard. You hear him muttering, "We shall fight winter on the hull, we shall fight winter on the teak, we shall never surrender." Move over Churchill. He blows the ship's air horn for emphasis. Howlyard hides under the sofa.

Ralph the Reluctant Teen lurches downstairs in long johns, rubbing sleep from his eyes.

"Yo, Dad, what's the reveille about?" Eagerly the captain issues his spring call-to-arms.

"We're off to charge the yard today. Pick up a sander. Join the fray." Ralph stares at his father in stunned disbelief.

"There's snow on the ground." Then he sees the rags.

"I can't believe you, Mom. You're throwing out my best Grateful Dead T-shirt. It's a collector's item." He rescues the rags and eyes you with utter teenage disgust.

"I'm going back to bed." As usual you are the only troop to be mustered.

It's not that you object to working on the boat. In fact you rather enjoy it when the yard is full of people, birds are singing and flowers blooming, the water is turned on, and the marina head is working. Particularly when the head is working. The nearest gas station is five miles away. But that is not the way it is going to be.

At moments like this it is easy to drag your feet a bit and suggest that you really ought to visit your mother. However ChapWoman advises you that this is no time to defect. Follow the captain into battle. You need the buddy system in boatyards in March. If he falls off the ladder, there won't be anybody around to get help. Like nine-year-old boys and second lieutenants, captains believe they are impervious to danger. Only women and children fall off ladders. Remember, there is compensation to this kind of chauvinism. You get the lifeboats first.

You arrive at the yard and are immediately buffeted by a stiff north wind. Its icy fingers grip you in a chilling embrace as you pick your way through the frozen ruts of mud amid a dismal landscape of hulls. Your captain always said he'd know *Mischief* anywhere, but quite frankly in a deserted marina one boat looks pretty much like another.

It pleases you to discover that when put to the test he does not race to her with arms outstretched while imaginary music serenades their reunion. Instead he stares myopically at each name on the transom.

Finally it is you, not he, who spots her in the far corner of the yard. The last time you saw her she was riding gently at anchor with her halyards singing joyously in the wind. Today she lies with her bottom exposed, looking strangely naked strapped to a cradle. She seems more like somebody recovering from surgery than the proud vessel you know her to be. Her halyards do not sing. They shriek at you to go home before you freeze to death.

There is snow in the cockpit. Muddy boots from the yard have streaked her decks with grime. The gulls have left their mark. She is definitely down on her luck.

So are you. There is no water in the yard, and the nearest electrical outlet is a block away. Perhaps the captain has not brought enough extension cord. Perhaps you can go home. But of course you can't because he has.

Once reunited with his beloved, he pats her bottom eagerly and hugs her bow with unabashed fervor. Beauty is definitely in the eye of the beholder, which makes you think twice about his taste in feminine beauty. You'd better go home and look in the mirror.

You think also about the $400 of antifouling bottom paint that stands between you and launch and of course you think

Beauty is in the eye of the beholder.

about the new upholstery for your living room sofa that stands
between you and sofa stuffing all over the floor. And you
know as you have always known that once again you will
patch the sofa with bookbinding tape. Maybe next year. Your
mother always told you it's the family who suffers when the
man is keeping his mistress in satin and furs.

And then in the midst of his reunion he steps back in alarm.
He has seen THEM. He races to the car for his knife and
begins poking at the proud blue underbelly already pocked
with pimples. Blisters.

You shudder. It is going to be a worse March than usual.
You will stand shoulder to shoulder with knives and epoxy
and sander operating on blisters. He will cut and fill and sand
and prime and you will make as many trips to the car as
possible so you can turn on the heat for 30 seconds.

Now that your captain has discovered the dread blisters he
will fret and fuss and discuss. Acne was nothing compared
with this. Like Mr. Gallup himself he will canvass the nation
to discover their cause. Is it better to leave a boat with blisters
in the water or out of the water? Nobody agrees. Start over,
they say—have the whole bottom redone for thousands of
dollars. You are not a religious woman but you do pray over

that one. The whole downstairs will be patched in bookbinding tape. Given the alternative you willingly devote your weekends to cutting and filling and sanding and wishing the head were working.

ChapWoman knows that there are couples who do not spend March in the mud in the do-it-yourself yard. They are the lucky ones who hire the marina to assault the ravages of winter. They arrive in early May with matched canvas bags, brass weather stations, and needlepoint cushions with ducks on them. They wear pressed white pants and party on the dock. They look nautically natty. You wear mud-splattered jeans, ragged sweatshirt, and a mask and look like a fugitive from germ warfare. You are unbelievably filthy.

Yes, you envy them, but you know you will never be one of them. Your captain believes that getting there is half the fun. Which is why you are wearing a mask and scraping and sanding until all of you is covered with blue paint chips. This year the environmentalists have banned the antifouling paint that is making you a candidate for a prime part in *Night of the Living Dead*. They say it is toxic to fish. You try not to think about what something that is toxic to fish has been doing to you for all these years.

But on the last work weekend you bring back the upholstery, paint the bottom a becoming blue, touch up the stripe, and stick a daffodil in the pulpit. The snow is gone, the birds are singing, the head is working, and all your friends are back working on their boats. You feel smug because your work is done. You are ready for launch. Maybe that robin wasn't so foolish after all.

pril

April is always the month you leave town. Sure, the captain's body goes through the motions of going to work but his heart and mind have gone to sea. *Mischief* is back in the water and he's itching to get away from it all, which means that you will spend the next 32 weekends on the lam. The captain will insist that anybody who has the temerity to be born, marry, or die during boating season is inconsiderate and couldn't possibly expect him to be present. You will reject all invitations and reschedule holidays and birthdays to Wednesdays. You have few friends left by fall.

This year the first of April falls on Friday, and your captain comes whistling home from the office at noon. April Fools', you hope. No such luck. It's time for spring commissioning, and he wants to get an early start.

Howlyard, the sea dog, shares his master's delight over the April exodus to the boat. He prances up and down the cellar steps, dogging the captain's footsteps and yapping until the captain produces his boat harness. Alas, your vision of Howlyard standing erect and proud in the bow of your boat, a canine Victory at Samothrace, vanishes. He lies on the floor, back paws waving wildly, writhing in ecstasy. Howlyard is a blithering idiot.

While master and dog trot back and forth to the car with life jackets, charts, dinghy oars, teak oil, charcoal grill, and sail bags you are at work on your big book of lists.

Moses had it easier getting the Jews out of Egypt. After all, they got to eat milk and honey and manna from heaven. All you can count on from heaven is a lightning bolt.

You need catsup and mustard; sugar and coffee and tea; crackers and cookies; spices and crab boil; peanut butter; Adolf's meat tenderizer for nettle stings; tonic and sodas and all the other things you will carefully stow and never find until fall. To say nothing of the sheets, blankets, and towels. You feel a warm kinship with the stewards on the *QE II*.

No, packing for the boat is not your favorite chore. You have never been one of those tidy, organized types who, before packing, multiplies number of people by number of sandwiches by slices of bread. Nor do you fill your ice chest with neatly labeled Tupperware bowls. Unfortunately, the food you stow in the bottom of the chest in the dark of night is usually what you will need for breakfast. There lies the butter buried in the bowels of the chest under boulders of ice. You need a miner's light and ear muffs to tunnel down to it.

Finally the sail locker is empty. Howlyard catapults into the back seat of the car with enthusiasm. You take your usual spot wedged between the genny and the lifesling with the charcoal grill in your lap. Each time the captain puts on the brakes an oar hits you in the head. They may have to carry you out on a stretcher.

When you arrive at the marina, the parking lot is full. You are obviously not the only April fools.

In spite of what the captain may claim, a marina is not a place to go to get away from it all. All of it is right smack on top of you—particularly on those first warm weekends of spring. Talk of your huddled masses. Whole families and dogs are packed into spaces the size of your front hall. There's considerably more privacy at the Boy Scout Jamboree.

Total strangers peer inquisitively down your companionway and marina mates peek into each other's portholes. They aren't peeping Toms. It's just that the boats are 24 inches apart and the curtains aren't up yet.

This is no haven for a hermit. But no sooner has the captain welded himself to a wheelbarrow than he undergoes a major personality change. Old Mr. Want-To-Be-Alone has turned into Mr. Congeniality. The grimace has become a grin. The same man who refused to buy Girl Scout cookies from a pig-tailed charmer and who went out the back door to avoid the new neighbor collecting for the heart fund is dispensing cheerful greetings and handshakes like a politician running for election.

He slaps Harry from New Jersey on the back and asks him how he made it through the winter.

"Didn't," Harry grins sheepishly. His wife Shirley looks pained. Seems that Harry and Shirley went shopping for an autopilot at the boat show and bought a 40-foot cutter instead.

"Two sails up front instead of one and no autopilot," mutters Shirley, who thought she'd spend the summer vegging

Marina mates peek into each other's portholes.

out with a good book instead of handling the helm. Suddenly it seems as if you got off easy with a spinnaker.

Himself is off to look at Harry's new boat. En route he spots Bill and Marge on A dock and invites them over for a drink as soon as he finds where you put the gin. Of course, Harry and Shirley are invited too, and Pete and Helen from the neighboring slip.

So you all crowd into *Mischief's* cockpit and pass plates of hors d'oeurves, which must be kept in perpetual motion since there isn't anywhere to put them down. Howlyard sits in the cockpit thumping his tail hopefully and waiting for a handout or the plate to drop—whichever comes first. The trawler across the dock has its stereo on high, two dogs are barking at each other, and a couple on C dock begins harmonizing to "Down By the Old Millstream." You listen in bemused wonder as your captain turns to Harry and says that he's been waiting all winter for the "peace and quiet" of the sailing life.

At sunup you grab your towel and soap and sprint down the dock hoping to hit the head before 70 others with the same

. . . and he said he needed a boat to get away from it all.

idea. No luck. They need the Go Patrol here. The traffic is backed up onto A dock because Alma from *Chapter 11* has chosen this moment to wash and coif her hair and that of her two daughters. By the time the family emerges in matching pink sweatshirts you are discussing intimate family secrets with the unshaven stranger behind you.

Harry rescues you from the usual April morning misery of cleaning the water tanks and anointing the packing glands with disgusting waterproof grease. He wants to take you for a spin in his new boat.

As you come aboard, Shirley is already up on the bow untying the docklines and waving to friends. Pete, your neighbor, swinging about in his boatswain's chair 50 feet up in the air, keeps shouting at you and pointing. You can't hear what he's saying.

"Must be admiring the boat," says Harry—the proud parent. He gives Pete a snappy salute. Pete does not salute back. He continues to yell and gesture.

"Better get him down—he's having some kind of fit," says Harry. ChapWoman would suggest that pride goeth before a fall. You go below and notice that you still have shore power.

It is then that you know what was on Pete's mind. You are 20 feet from the dock with a long yellow umbilical cord stretched out across the water.

At moments like this your marina mates pop out on deck like flowers in spring. It's entertainment time. Harry says loudly that none of this would have happened if the mate had done her job instead of gallivanting on the bow. Shirley says that any captain worth his salt would know whether he was unplugged or plugged unless he was too busy showing off. The atmosphere topside is formal.

But all is quickly forgotten when Harry comes about into the wind and your captain raises the main and kills the engine. At first the cloak of silence wraps you in its folds. Then you listen again to the individual sounds of boat, wind, and water —the swoosh of the breeze filling the sails; the flap-flap when Harry comes about; the grinding and squeak of the winches; the slap of the waves against the hull and the mournful clang of the bell buoy guarding the rocks; the thunk of lines on the deck, and the strident screech of gulls circling a fishing boat nearby. As always it is your favorite symphony—the music of sailing. The sky stretches blue and cloudless overhead and you feel the first whisper-warm caress of sun on your back. Alas, your captain is oblivious to the poetry of wind and water. Like a kid in a candy store he is mesmerized by Harry's integrated instrument system.

Although Harry's boat is strange, your body adjusts easily to the heel. Your four landlubbing months are over. Although there will still be several more weekends of elbow grease before *Mischief* is ready to take off down the bay, it is nice to be reminded of the light at the end of the tunnel.

You're back in time for the paintshed party. Now, an April party in a clammy, unheated paintshed is not for everyone. The ambience is early warehouse and the menu is always the same although nobody plans it. It is one of the mysteries of boating that year after year half the mates bring chili and the other half bring macaroni or bean salad.

The captains, resplendent in ski parkas and watch caps, clap each other on the back and cluster together like long lost family members from behind the Iron Curtain. Of winter, that is. They chatter on about rigging and marinas and whether the harbor was dredged and where to put a spinnaker halyard. Forget about the market and taxes and interest rates.

This is the conversation that counts. Down here in the paint-shed chowing down on chili the captain's most pressing concern is what direction the wind is blowing tomorrow. That's what getting away from it is all about.

May

May is the captain's month. The wind is up, the sun is warm, and the bay is dotted with sails. Best of all, the brightwork is behind you, along with the Bligh side of the captain's disposition. The peace, panic, and endurance of the sailing life are about to begin. But not the way you'd hoped.

"Walt and his wife are coming to the boat this weekend," announces the captain.

"Ugh—customers. On our *first sail* of the season?"

"Boating is good for business," chants the captain. It is his spring mantra.

You remind him of Leroy who stamped out cigarettes on the cockpit sole, David who wrapped himself up in the spinnaker, and of course, Blakeley Martin's son who tried to unscrew the through-hull fittings.

"It's not fair to subject *Mischief* to customers. Keelhauling would be too good for that dreadful Martin kid."

"But remember Blakeley's wife," he smiles dreamily. You'll never forget her: thirty years younger than Blakeley, wearing a string bikini and coaxing the captain to teach her celestial. She's a good reason to cool it with customers. Customers are a grab bag. You never know what's coming down the dock. It might be Blakeley's wife or it might be reluctant Reba Gottwall. She wears a shapeless college sweatshirt and gobbles seasick pills. She never looks back when her feet touch shore again. So you suggest taking Walt and wife to dinner and a show.

"Boating is a better ambience," he says.

Yes, customers are different from friends or crew. Crew knows what it is doing and is either up on the foredeck setting the spinnaker or down at the chart table plotting the course and checking the tide tables. Crew is a joy.

Friends are okay, too. They don't know as much as crew but are eager to learn. They help in the galley, sun on the foredeck, and do their own thing.

Customers are prima donnas who come from a world of bright lights, big cities, and concrete. They don't lift a finger to help. You are their crew. They expect to be entertained. The husband wants a "water experience" to talk about in the office. The wife wants to stay home. So do you.

You are down below when *Mischief* lurches. Walt has arrived—all 250 pounds of him. He has also walked across a dock paved with seagull droppings. You ask him if he would mind taking off his brand new boat shoes. He withers you with a look. He would mind. He is used to giving orders, not taking them. He strides forcefully across the deck, leaving a trail of gull behind, and allows the captain a photo opportunity at the helm. You follow discreetly with a rag.

Walt has a cigar clamped in his teeth, a Lacoste shirt, knife-sharp creases in his white pants, binoculars around his neck, and a hard-sided suitcase.

"I never trust those canvas duffels: they don't lock," he says while you wonder with dismay where you will stow the suitcase—and what contraband he might have locked inside. Judging from the weight, it could be a dozen gold bricks.

Daisy, his wife, is one of those timid, pale types who says little and does her duty. She has memorized three responses to where she might like to go and what she might like to do: "I don't care," "That's okay," and "It doesn't matter to me." The only other information she volunteers is that her garden club tour was this weekend.

The captain goes below to give his usual speech on where to find the life jackets, what to do in case of fire, and how to operate the head.

"If you don't keep the handle up and the pedal forward we will sink." Daisy shudders. You've always thought he lacked finesse.

He says that a little hyperbole makes a point. Daisy won't forget now. She won't use the head either.

Nothing is secret or sacred on a boat. After dinner ashore you make up the main salon for Walt and Daisy and retire to the vee-berth. Daisy says she is going to take a shower. The head door closes behind her. Silence. You wait. You do not hear water.

"What the hell are you doing in there?" growls Walt. You strain to hear Daisy's answer. No water runs. Nothing flushes. After a while she comes out again. You settle down for sleep.

Sometime in the middle of the night you are awakened by the sound of pigs rooting in the garbage, followed by an eerie whistle and more pigs. Dazed, you sit up. Where are you? Alas, you remember. It is only the beginning of the weekend. Walt is snoring. Daisy rolls him over. Daisy wakes him up. Walt goes back to sleep. Daisy actually says "shut up." Walt snores on. How does she stand it?

In the morning you leap from the vee-berth at the first mutter in the salon. Walt and Daisy have separated you from your coffee pot.

"Good morning," you trill, ever the enthusiastic camp counselor. Nobody looks happy. The reality of a night on board sleeping on the dining room table is a far cry from a nonboater's cruise ship expectations. Walt complains that the bed was too hard and too cramped and the marina too noisy. He didn't sleep a wink. You stare at him in disbelief.

Daisy is sitting bleary-eyed on the settee in a house coat, holding a towel and clutching a roll of toilet paper to her bosom. She is a pathetic sight. She is going to shower in the marina head. Seems she didn't take a shower on board. She just sat there mesmerized by the spigots, not remembering which to turn and fearful that sinking might be only a spigot away.

It is going to be a long day. Daisy settles down topside after breakfast for the customer's predictable game of 20 questions. Her eyes dart desperately about the cockpit. She points to winches, halyards, snatch blocks, traveler, and lines. Over and over she asks, "What's that? What does it do?" "What's that? What does it do?" Your answers sound like the Basic Boating text. It is the lowest form of human communication— just one step away from "me Tarzan, you Jane."

And since *Mischief* is well appointed, it could continue all morning. Daisy goes below to retrieve her sunglasses.

"I'd get seasick downstairs," she says. You don't bother to correct her. Instead you beam at this newfound opportunity. "Don't mind me," you say, "I'm going to have to spend some time in the galley." You escape to your pots, leaving Daisy's further education to the captain.

Walt, of course, is a helm hog. Once he has his hands on the wheel he won't let go. This is what he came for. Just wait 'til he tells the guys at the office that he took over the ship. Considering that the harbor is full of crab pots, the captain does not want him to take over the ship. Dodging pots is not for neophyte sailors, particularly when the wind is up and the pots vanish in the trough.

Walt, of course, is a helm hog.

"I'll take the helm 'til we get out of the crab farm," orders the captain. Walt stiffens. He does not take orders. Instead he grips the wheel and stares straight ahead. "What's the big deal? This is a piece of cake." You wait. Nobody disobeys the captain on *Mischief*. Nobody but a customer, that is.

"I'll spot for you," says the captain through clenched teeth.

"Black one to port; take it downwind . . . look out for the red one—you're right on it—turn a bit to starboard." Unable to follow so many instructions at once, Walt plows into the

29

pot. The captain grabs the wheel and shuts off the engine. Walt instantly discharges any responsibility by yelling for Daisy.

"Daisy, where were you? *Mischief* hit a pot." Daisy is sitting two feet away from him knitting.

"Oh dear, I'm so sorry." Obviously it is a Pavlovian response.

"We'll have to dive for it," says the captain grimly. The water is still cold in May. Walt clears up the "we'll" bit right away.

"Damn shame I can't help, old man, got a bit of a sore throat coming on," he says, coughing for emphasis. It is the first and last cough of the day.

The captain dives and dives. He is turning blue. Daisy is animated. When *Mischief* is finally free, she gives a pattering of applause. Perhaps she thinks this is Sea World.

Now that the emergency is past, Walt sidles back behind the helm. Too cold to question, the captain leaves you in charge and goes below to get some hot soup.

"How cold do you have to be before you die from hypothermia?" asks Daisy.

Walt is just as oblivious to the dangers of hypothermia as he was to the crab pots. All he's interested in now is checking the chart and the markers. He preens a bit after sailing in a straight line from the channel marker to the buoy marking the entrance to the river.

"Nothing to navigation," he says. You bite your tongue before adding that anybody can sail from point A to point B on a bright sunny day when you can see both marks. Unless, of course, you are blind.

But now that Walt is an expert, he's going to ignore the wisdom of the charts.

"Pretty silly to take such an out of the way jog to that nun when you can sail straight to the day marker by cutting a bit."

"There's thin water over there," you say, but by then everybody knows there is thin water. *Mischief* lurches to a halt.

"Daisy—where are you?" howls Walt.

You are not sorry to bid farewell to Walt and Daisy in Annapolis. They have decided to spend Saturday night ashore. Later you sit in *Mischief's* cockpit enjoying the lighted harbor and glad that at last you are alone. The only jarring note is the continual sound of the captain sneezing.

June

Racing was certainly easier to take when the captain denied he was doing it. Don't ever believe a sailor who looks you straight in the eye and declares stoutly: "I'm a cruiser, not a racer." Be aware at once that you are looking at a person who is deluding himself badly.

All sailors race. There doesn't have to be an official course, or a starting gun, or buoys to round. Ragmen are simply incapable of sitting in a boat for more than 30 seconds without glancing about to see if there isn't another vessel in sight to catch up with, pass, or stay ahead of.

As soon as he hoists the mainsail and puts his hand on the tiller, watch how the Old Sea Dog's head goes up, his nostrils quiver, his whole body tenses. Right then you know the chase is on!

But of course, there's a ritual involved. Once an opponent is sighted, an immediate change takes place. Now the captain lolls in the cockpit, pretending complete indifference. He glances neither to port nor starboard, appearing to snooze behind his Polaroid shades.

Actually, hawklike, he is watching an approaching boat out of the corner of his eye, while at the same time silently calculating how to close the distance between himself and the boat ahead of him. Of course, the captain of the boat ahead of him is doing the same thing.

The tension mounts. However, the mate may be completely unaware this duel of wits is in progress. It's sort of difficult to know that a race is taking place because in actual fact the rate of speed is generally so slow that the time taken in passing another boat averages one to three hours.

During this endless rite of passage, the mates on the two boats may become fast friends, exchanging confidences and recipes while the skippers stare straight ahead as though they are alone on the bay. If they do enter into communication, it's with a small wave of the hand and a surprised look that says, "Why, where did you come from?" All the while they're craftily maneuvering for the racer's edge.

The mates on the two boats become fast friends, exchanging recipes and confidences.

But this summer is going to be different. Your captain announces that you will be racing for real. Your Bay Sailing Association has initiated a summer and fall racing series. Bligh buys a stopwatch and an incredibly boring video called *The Shape of Sail*. It's okay for him to watch, but he wants you there, too. He mutters about racing spinnakers and drifters. It is time to take stock of the situation. No more leisurely cruising or gunkholing for you. You'll be spending your weekends as sewerman.

Now, when you go sailing, your captain cares about blanket zones and how to get into a safe leeward position. He carries the Rule Book of the United States Yacht Racing Union next to his heart and is mouthing off rule numbers, not the rules.

"My God, you've broken 38.1," he bellows and you cringe with shame and grab the rule book to see what you did. You get him later when you mention that he'd better watch out for Appendix 10, Rule 22.3.

The first and hardest part of the race usually takes place on land. It involves the question of logistics. How can six people, living in four houses in two states, converge on dock C two hours away at the same time with enough food and beer for a given race afternoon?

The captain calls all members of the crew the night before the race. He sent them maps and memos earlier in the week. The crew must not get lost, stop for breakfast, get hung up in road construction or, God forbid, be one second late. Bud, the navigator, is apologetic. His wife has gone into labor. The captain allots Bud's wife 12 hours.

He rolls you out of bed and onto the road at five a.m. He begins pacing the dock at nine. His blood pressure rises until, at last, Bud arrives bleary-eyed. The captain hoists the sails without asking if it's a boy or a girl.

The race doesn't start for another hour, but the captain feels that the secret of a racer's success is an early start. He sails over to the committee boat to check the course and get a read on the wind direction. Of course the wind will change before race time. He decides which end of the start is favored by the wind. Of course the wind will change by race time. He checks the sail to be sure it is right for these conditions. Of course these conditions will change by race time. He runs off at the starting line and times the amount of time it takes to get back to it. It gives him a nice bit of nautical theory, but of course the wind will change by race time.

While all this busywork is going on, Bud keeps trying to tell somebody he had a boy and that his wife is resting comfortably.

ChapWoman would remind you that if yachting is the sport of gentlemen, racing is the sport of intimidation. A lifetime of good manners will vanish in a single race afternoon. Scowling skippers push and shove, barge and butt in front of other boats. Nobody takes turns or says "after you" as they round the marks. Instead they steal each other's wind and then laugh coarsely.

Nothing in your past training has prepared you for the disorder of crossing a starting line with 22 other boats. They are all trying to converge into an area smaller than the neck of an hourglass at a precise second in time.

As one boat comes about, tacking directly in front of you, another sweeps your stern so closely that you duck to avoid being hit by its boom. With 15 seconds to the starting gun, Pete, the fleet captain, whom you always considered the perfect gentleman, forces you to luff up. They'd never do anything like that at the New York Yacht Club. Not all those good-looking men in their navy blazers and red pants. You plan to mention this fact to Pete later tonight. But first you plan to have him spend the remainder of the afternoon watching your wake.

In the midst of pandemonium the starting gun goes off and shortly afterwards the breeze dies out. It seems to do that quite often in races. The captain and his crew spend several hours bouncing up and down in the wake of fishing boats. Bud has retired below and snores gently. The white handkerchief you hung from the backstay as a racing flag is an embarrassment. Powerboaters skim past, demolishing the little headway you had managed to attain. The sun beats down on your head. You want to put up the bimini. The captain refuses. He claims it will slow your speed. Since you haven't moved forward in over an hour, you wonder how seriously the sun has affected him.

And speaking of wondering, where has the rest of the fleet gotten to? You see a few of them, well up ahead, ghosting along in the faintest whisper of a breeze near the opposite shore—the shore your captain has said would be blanketed.

You go below to check on Bud and review the racing rules. Prohibited actions include: sculling, pumping, and ooching. Now frankly, you have always been of the decided opinion that a little ooching never hurt anybody.

Then the wind returns. A cat's-paw, it advances toward you, ruffling the water, slowly filling the sail. It lifts the damp hair from your brow, and the slump from your spirit. You are back in the race!

You cross the finish line sometime after the other competitors have completed their course, their showers, and their first round of drinks on the yacht club porch. The captain and crew congratulate each other as you all head for shore. You may not be able to brag much at the party tonight, but your boat finished the race. And there's always next Saturday. You raise a glass of the bubbly to Bud's boy, Bill, and send Dad on his way.

ChapWoman has compiled a list for the Novice Racing Mate aboard the Novice Racing Vessel:

1) Keep your eyes and ears open at the cocktail party on the evening preceding the Big Event. Find out who is

Keep your eyes and ears open at the cocktail party.

supposed to win the race and the name of his/her boat. Next morning, as soon as the 10 minute warning flag is hoisted, urge your captain to get on that boat's tail and stay there, following closely in her wake right across the finishing line.

2) Remember that a screw, washer, or cotter pin tossed on an opponent's foredeck on the morning of the race gives the vessel's captain and crew something to think about, and in the spirit of camaraderie, helps divert their attention from the arduous race ahead. (Pete, the fleet captain, could use that sort of distraction next Saturday.)

3) Remind your captain that a team nattily dressed in brand new matching yachting outfits gives real snap to the boat's appearance and is likely to impress the race committee at the finish line.

4) Be aware of the old nautical maxim: Maneuvering around the starting line five minutes before the race is not for the faint of heart.

5) Be on your guard when confronted with a sailboat being towed to the starting line. This does not neces-

sarily imply engine failure. What you may have here is a captain who empties his water and fuel tanks to lighten his boat for the race. Be careful of him. He undoubtedly means business and is a hard-nosed racer.

6) Be aware that during the race the rules of courtesy and etiquette employed by the captain toward the crew often follow the guidelines laid down by Genghis Khan.

7) In a situation where you feel you have the legitimate right of way, the cry "starboard tack" does not win for you the respect that a bellowed "steel hull" does.

8) Understand that the order of finish has absolutely nothing to do with the final results of the race. In yachting, the race is not always to the swift nor the battle to the strong. Sometimes you'll find that the PHRF handicaps give a nautical twist to the story of the hare and the tortoise.

9) A protest may be lodged by any yacht against another yacht who has supposedly infringed a rule of racing against her. If a captain waves a red flag at you, he believes he has been fouled. The protest meeting following the race is reminiscent of a senate investigation and when it is all over, the race committee will disqualify both boats. However, the captain who remains for the dinner afterwards has won a moral victory.

July

The captain stands on *Mischief's* bow inhaling the salt air and gazing out at the Atlantic Ocean. He's about to cut loose and make like Chichester, Slocum, or a Viking captain. Scratch Viking captain. They were buried with their ships. Burial at sea is the last thing you want to think about on the eve of your yearly voyage to New England by the outside.

The captain has corralled a crew of three. Block Island, Cuttyhunk, and Martha's Vineyard are the carrot on the stick he dangled in front of them. He says little about the 48 hours on the ocean.

It isn't as easy to get crew as it used to be. Your friends have heard about the freighter that almost gutted you in the Ambrose shipping channel, the rogue wave that swept over you, filling the cockpit and cabin with water, and of course, Bill's wife Helen has told a few friends that she didn't appreciate being called short, fat, and stupid while trying to hold up the boom that had fallen on her head.

Helen has lost a few pounds and forgiven the captain but refuses to sail with him. Bill, however, has agreed to give you a hand as far as Block Island. Just when you've given up hope of having any more crew than Bill, the captain comes home grinning. Chuck, the new man in his department, knows how to sail. His bride does not.

"Newlyweds—just what I need," chortles the captain. "Once we get to Block we'll make this the Love Boat: full moon, violin music, and all that." You hate to burst his bubble, but it may take more than violins after 48 hours at sea.

You've never seen them before, but you know with a sinking feeling that the couple holding hands and ambling across the dock is your crew. She is wearing natty white pants and a navy blazer with lots of brass buttons. She is also carrying a glass casserole dish and a make-up case.

She remains cool, polite, and distant while Chuck is all over the boat, enthusiastically pumping the captain's hand and any other hand in sight and thanking you again and again for the invitation. He introduces his wife, whose name is Kitten.

Now it will be your job to make Kitten comfortable. It may not be easy.

She is incredulous when you explain that offshore you will all sleep in the main salon.

"Isn't that a bit cozy?"

"Oh, we keep our clothes on," you stumble on. *Mischief's* honor must be upheld. She is not a swinging boat.

"There isn't much room, is there?" After that, life below seems a bit squalid even to you—particularly when you explain that she may need to suck the sink for water pressure.

Topside, Kitten motions to Chuck to come up on the bow. They are "having words." Couples having words all look alike. Although you cannot hear them, you can imagine her begging Chuck to get off now before it is too late. Chuck is shaking his head. So much for the Love Boat.

Oblivious to the strained silence in the cockpit, the captain bounces on board with steamed lobsters. Those lobsters snuggled together in their carton probably knew each other a lot better than you know your crew. It's always like that at the beginning of a cruise, but ChapWoman has noticed that something happens out there on the ocean and strangers become soulmates. Perhaps Kitten will be the exception.

"This is the thing that writers write about and sailors sing about," enthuses the captain as he drinks in the sea air and pitches the lobster shells into the briny deep.

Mischief cuts through gentle seas while the sun sets in a bonfire of red and gold, licking away the clouds in a final fiery blaze until all that remains are dying purple embers. The lights of New Jersey twinkle behind you and the vast canopy of stars stretches overhead. Cares and concerns from home vanish in the limitless expanse of sea and sky. But your concern about Kitten and Chuck stays with you.

The captain gives his usual speech about conserving water because *Mischief* carries only 30 gallons.

"Each of you gets half a cup a day—wash first, then you can drink it." It's his little joke but you are afraid Kitten believes him. She moves to the far side of the boat and glares at Chuck. Her eyes remain riveted to the vanishing shoreline. The end of her life or her marriage—whichever comes first—is in sight.

The captain hands out crew assignments. Chuck will navigate, Bill will handle the sails. Everybody will take their turn standing watch.

"Two hours on and three hours off," says the captain.

"All night and all day?" blurts Kitten in disbelief. Perhaps Chuck didn't level with her about this trip. Men tend to gloss over the nitty-gritty when they want to go sailing. It's time for the chicken soup. At times like this you always bring on the chicken soup to remind the crew of a happier time.

Captain Cupid insists that Chuck and Kitten take the first watch, although Kitten looks like she'd rather stand watch with a gorilla. But the first watch is the best and certainly the most romantic. The boat is still dry, the air is warm, and the moon washes a glittering moonpath in front of *Mischief*. The rest of you go below, and once when you peek on deck Chuck has his arm around Kitten and she has her head on his shoulder.

"See," the captain nudges you, "we'll have a crew for next year after all." Perhaps he is jumping the gun. One cuddle does not a crewman make.

Romantic they may have been, but they are also off course. One minute you are dozing on the settee, lulled to sleep by the swish and swoosh of the waves as *Mischief* glides smoothly through the water. The next, *Mischief* is drunkenly lurching from port to starboard. Bill tumbles off the settee and rolls about the cabin sole. You feel queasy as *Mischief* lurches back to port. Sails are flapping, the captain is barking and Chuck is grabbing the wheel from Kitten who has been over-compensating to get back on the right compass heading. Her face is all puckered up and she's sniffing and about to burst into tears. That's the end of any romance.

When the agony of her third watch is over, her make-up is a memory along with her blazer. She wears Chuck's long underwear, an old grey sweater somebody left on the boat, Bill's watch cap, your foulweather gear, and a grim expression. She speaks to no one. But although she is bleary-eyed, cold, wet, and miserable, she now holds a compass course. She lumbers below, falls onto the settee, and is instantly asleep. She does not move for three hours. You wonder if she is clinically dead. Perhaps you will have to sit on her for breakfast.

Midmorning brings calm to the crew. Chuck puts way-points in the Loran, Bill and the captain hoist the spinnaker and Kitten, who has rejoined the living, is wearing her own clothes again but no make-up and mascara. The captain may have been correct that this is the thing that writers write about and sailors sing about.

But then in the late afternoon the wind picks up and the men douse the spinnaker. The seas are building steadily to six to ten feet. A 30-knot wind slices the tops off the waves and hurls ribbons of spray over the boat.

Kitten cowers in her corner. *Mischief* forges ahead under power, scaling each wave then falling with a crash into the trough below. Salt spray washes over the deck and everything that isn't tied down crashes about in the cabin. Including Chuck. He had been taking a nap until Mother Nature decided to liven things up a bit and fling a tea kettle across the cabin at him.

The captain gets out the safety harnesses and clamps Kitten to the stanchion. She clenches her teeth and grips the winch until her knuckles are as white as her face. Until now you have wondered what naked fear looked like.

"I'm afraid she'll divorce Chuck the minute we get to Block," you whisper to the captain, who looks worried himself. He tries for a bit of jocularity.

"Nothing like crashing to windward to clear the soul," he shouts over the roar of the surf. He looks quite mad.

"*Mischief* has come through a lot worse storms than this," you reassure Kitten while discreetly covering the windspeed indicator, which just hit 40. A tear trickles down Kitten's nose.

"We're going to be washed overboard," she sobs. The captain, never known for his sensitivity, chooses this moment to show Kitten how to work the flares on the life jacket. Before you can kick him he adds, "Just a precaution in case you go overboard." Kitten's eyes are squeezed tight shut. She is saying the rosary.

The wind finally drops at dawn and your bruised and battered band spots the Long Island shoreline and the comforting sight of fishing boats and the Montauk light.

"You can open your eyes now, Kitten. We can see Block Island," says Chuck, and for just a minute you think she might swim for it.

You go below to survey the wreckage in the cabin. Lester Jeter never lived like this. Food, clothing, books, life jackets, foulweather gear, sweaters, seaboots, cushions, and the long forgotten make-up case litter the cabin sole, along with the blue blazer, which Bill rolled up and used for a pillow.

She flags the fishing fleet by waving her red bikini in the air.

But that's not all there is on the floor. There's water. Lots and lots of water. You don't think Kitten can take much more so you beckon the captain and whisper, "I think we're sinking."

"WHAT DO YOU MEAN SINKING?" he yells back. As noted before, he is not a sensitive man.

But you needn't have worried about Kitten. She has beaten the grim reaper, lived to see the dawn, survived a storm at sea, and seen land. She has become a new kind of cat. She takes immediate charge of the situation by donning a life jacket and rushing to the bow where she stands in the pulpit like a Viking masthead. She waves her arms, screams "Help," and finally flags the fishing fleet by waving her red bikini in the air. She is a magnificent sight with blond hair blowing in the breeze. The fishing fleet agrees and rushes to the rescue at the same time the captain discovers that the hot water tank is leaking. The disappointed fleet continues to tag along, waving to Kitten and hoping she will abandon ship.

As soon as the anchor is set in the Great Salt Pond you go ashore. The color that drained out of Kitten's face two days ago has returned. She has looked positively perky since rounding up the fishing fleet with her red bikini.

Block Island is a culture shock after two days at sea. The ferry has just arrived and the pier is swarming with men and

41

women in straw hats. A band is playing Dixieland jazz. You stop to listen and are almost bisected by a bicycle. If it weren't necessary to give the crew shore leave, the captain would never leave his ship.

But today he has a purpose. He steers Kitten and Chuck to a romantic, vine-covered patio facing the sea and urges them to have a drink under a brightly striped umbrella while you take Bill to the airport. By the time you return they are cuddling and cocooning.

"Praise the Lord," says the captain, wiping the perspiration from his brow.

After a day on Block you set sail for Cuttyhunk. The water is crystal clear, the sky a cloudless blue, and the sun warm. Kitten snoozes with Chuck on the foredeck looking better wearing a bikini than waving it. The only emergency is avoiding being hit by the seaplane.

After hot showers at the Allen Hotel the four of you explore Cuttyhunk's laurel-covered bluffs and Kitten picks a bunch of Queen Anne's lace, blue chicory, and bright orange trumpet vine. It's her peace offering to *Mischief*. Later that evening, warmed by friendship, you discuss the questions and quandaries of your lives and you feel as if you have known each other for a long time. Kitten even laughs about a captain who drinks his own bathwater and says she wishes she were a better sailor.

"We'll take care of that," gloats the captain, sitting in the catbird seat at last.

Kitten takes the helm when you set sail for Martha's Vineyard in the rose-fingered dawn. Chuck trims sails and the captain smiles paternally at his crew.

And then you feel a certain dank clamminess in the air. This is not the fog of romance writers; it does not tiptoe in on little cat feet. Instead with one great gulp it swallows you up like Audrey the plant in the Little Shop of Horrors.

One minute you're off the shoreline of Martha's Vineyard and the next you have a front row seat at *Vanish at Sea*. Houdini was a zero compared with this. Now you see the Vineyard; now it's gone. Now you see a large schooner and a larger ferry to port; now they are gone, although you hear an ominous booming where you think they ought to be. You wish you'd checked to see if the ferry was coming or going. The captain hopes it is going because you are coming.

The captain and Chuck are up on the bow with the foghorn. Kitten is up on the foredeck tossing potatoes.

You are at the helm thinking existential thoughts like the fact that nobody knows you are here, and you don't even know where here is or whether you will ever get to there.

Suddenly you hear a loud thump and a clang. You are definitely somewhere.

"What did you hit?" yells the captain, and then there is a second clang. You have hit a buoy. Which is doing its buoy thing a little late, you think.

"There isn't any wave motion on a foggy day. That's what makes a buoy work, so it keeps its mouth shut until you run into it. I learned that in physics," says Kitten, smiling broadly. She peers at the number.

"We're right where we belong; this buoy marks the harbor entrance."

"You've learned to read charts," says an awed captain.

Chuck has his arm around Kitten. "Who knows? Maybe next year Kitten and I will scuttle your ship."

That night the captain is euphoric. Glorious summers of cruising in New England and Maine stretch ahead. No more worry about crew.

"Nova Scotia, Denmark Strait," he mumbles in his sleep. Then he sits bolt upright in the vee-berth, banging his head.

"My God! What if she gets pregnant?"

ugust

The same things always happen in August. You wish they didn't. The days are hot, sultry, and moist with a blue heat haze floating over the marina. Newspapers report 10 deaths from the heat and doctors suggest staying inside air-conditioned houses. Many boats lie listlessly in their slips because their owners have heeded this warning. You, of course, are wiping the sweat from your brow, seeing mirages, and preparing to set sail.

In August the term "set sail" is a euphemism. The sail hangs limply from the mast while you lie limply on deck, too dehydrated to move. You and the bay and the dog are flat. The captain insists a breeze is coming.

Meanwhile the sun beats down on your head. Your brain fries and your skin turns brown and dies. It is too late for Retin A. But you are not alone in your misery. Howlyard the sea dog lies panting on the deck, fixing you with a sad, reproachful gaze. He's been boating in August before and knows the score. Today he was hiding in the basement behind the furnace before the captain flushed him out.

In August the greenheads dive-bomb you by day, and then at dusk whole regiments of mosquitoes descend on the deck. You zap everything in sight with bug spray, but still they whirrr and hum about your head, make sneak attacks on your bare arms, and join the gnats dancing around the candle. You blow out the candle, grope your dinner in the dark, swat and scratch and annoint yourself with bug repellent. Chanel No. 5 it is not.

It is only after you are in the vee-berth finally feeling smug with victory that you hear it—a sound louder than all the katydids on shore, louder than Howlyard snoring, louder than John Philip Sousa himself marching into town with drums and cymbals. It is one lone mosquito.

It circles your head, feasts on your cheek, returns for a chunk of the captain's ear. At this moment any resemblance between the captain and Humphrey Bogart poling the *African Queen* through crocodile-infested waters vanishes.

You and the bay and the dog are flat. The Ancient Mariner insists a breeze is brewing.

Humphrey may have made it without losing his cool, but your captain runs amok.

He thrashes about the vee-berth raving, swatting, cursing, and spraying. Then he charges into the cabin red-faced and stark naked, armed with a fly swatter. He is not a pretty sight.

Howlyard, acting on his fight or flight instinct, takes stock of the situation and flees to the foredeck. You follow suit. While the captain starts a one-man riot, you and Howlyard plan a break-out by dinghy.

In August the captain tells you he wants to look at the stars with you. Chapwoman knows what you're thinking: moonlight, romance, a glass of wine, and a cuddle in the cockpit. No such luck. He's into celestial navigation and must finish his sights by fall to pass the course. His mind is on the setting sun, not you.

He powers *Mischief* into the bay, drops anchor, and crouches on the foredeck with his sextant. You hold the stopwatch, not his hand. He has one eye on the horizon and the other on Arcturus and the big black cloud that is about to make Arcturus invisible. He is agitated. You write down min-

He is not a pretty sight.

utes and seconds. He talks of dip. It is hardly the language of love, particularly when the cloud moves in and you realize you are going to repeat the whole performance next weekend.

In August you have thunderstorms. Lots of them. And you worry about getting electrocuted, which is not something you think about during the rest of the year. Since your mother told you to get out of the bathtub at the first distant thunder rumble and to stay away from metal objects, you wonder why you are sitting in the middle of a large body of water with a tall metal mask sticking through the boat and a large metal steering wheel on deck.

The captain assures you that you have nothing to worry about because of something called the cone of protection. You cannot be electrocuted within a 60-degree angle from the tip of the mast. Terror-stricken that a stray finger or toe should protrude beyond the magic angle, you and Howlyard huddle in a ball in the corner of the cockpit with arms and paws around each other. It's a good thing for humanity that Ben Franklin had a kite, a key, and curiosity. All you have is fear.

This year your sister Beth is coming in August. Something always breaks when Beth comes, which is why she has renamed *Mischief* "Murder at Sea." Last summer it was the transmission. You were in the shipping channel and it was touch-and-go who would get to you first—the Coast Guard or the Liberian freighter. The year before the heat exchanger cracked, spewing water and carbon monoxide into the cabin. That same day the shower blew apart and the swim ladder broke.

Beth warns you that this will be a working vacation—she has one chapter still to write on her dissertation. The captain greets her joyously and chivalrously offers her a hand aboard with her laptop, in its waterproof carrying case. At first you think he is really beginning to like your family. He tells Beth that she is looking trim. You beam. Beth preens. "Light as a feather," he says. Ah, vanity. She isn't really paying attention when he says that she is so light that he wonders if she'd do him a tiny little favor and run up the mast to fix the wind indicator. He makes it sound like running to the market. "Sure," she says. Has she forgotten she's afraid of heights?

So when you put down the lunchhook, the captain winches Beth up the mast. She remembers. There she is 50 feet in the air and clinging to the mast like some kind of primitive life form when the captain announces that the anchor is dragging. No need to bring her down just to winch her up again.

"Hang on," he shouts. She can't respond because her vocal cords have frozen. By the time the captain settles on a new spot her fingers are clamped about the mast like a Vise-Grip. You will have to call the fire department to get her down.

When at last she is back on deck she goes below to the safety of her dissertation. *Mischief* slats about in the grilling midday heat until unexpectedly a breeze ruffles the water. "See," says the captain, "we'll have a good sail after all."

"See," you say, pointing to the horrible greenish-black clouds gathering behind you. "We'd better go back to the slip while we still can."

"No way. We're meeting Harry and Bill tonight."

"Well . . . if I were the captain . . ."

You arrive at the anchorage and raft up with Harry and Bill. One minute you are settled on Harry's boat with drinks watching the storm hit somebody else; the next the thunder is booming and lightning is streaking the sky overhead. It is too late to break the raft apart. The storm that you've watched

Ben Franklin had a kite, a key, and curiosity. All you have is terror.

gathering and building all afternoon has whipped itself into a fury over your anchorage.

The wind shrieks and howls. You are pelted by rain and hail. The three boats swing wildly. Seconds after you and Beth seek shelter below, Bill shouts, "We're dragging!"

Beth gathers her laptop to her bosom while you get out the life jackets as a precaution. Precaution nothing. One look out the porthole tells you you may be using those jackets unless you are smashed to bits first on the dock full of very expensive boats that lies between you and land. Sheets of rain wash down the portholes. The raft speeds toward shore. Two boat owners are out on deck with drawn boathooks. You can't imagine what good they'll do. A third is gesturing wildly toward your captain and preparing to fling himself in front of your raft to protect his boat. ChapWoman has noticed that in extreme cases a captain will lay down his life for his boat.

This time you really do think the end is in sight. "I'm sorry I locked you in the cellar when you were six," you say to quivering Beth.

"I didn't mean to give your favorite doll to the toy drive at school," says Beth.

"You *what? . . .* " you shout over the crashing thunder. But you realize it doesn't really matter. Lightning zigzags toward you.

You're not going down without a fight. It's time to consider swimming. You drag Howlyard, Beth, and her laptop on deck. And then just as the wind wails, the rain stings, and you're getting ready to abandon ship you hear a new noise. It is the roar of engines. The three captains have gotten aboard their boats and put all the engines on full power in reverse. Within feet of a 52-foot fishing boat called *Branch Office* the raft reverses. You are close enough to see the owner, the same one who was preparing to fling himself between boat and raft. Now he falls to the deck on his knees and crosses himself. You are living proof that miracles exist.

Not long afterward the rain stops, the wind dies, and the storm continues on its way. Your dinghy is upside down, the oars are gone, and one of the cockpit cushions is in the water along with the captain's hat, but other than that there is very little damage to the boats.

There is, however, a little problem about the doll and the cellar. One tends to get loose-lipped when preparing to meet the grim reaper.

The captain pats you on the back. "You know, mate," he says, "You might have been right about going back to the slip today." Those words make the whole storm worthwhile.

Fresh, cool air follows nature's vengeance and even Beth feels better after a few glasses of wine and steak cooked on the grill. You sit in the cockpit listening to the deafening din of the katydid chorus and feel a momentary sadness for the day a month or so from now when the chorus is stilled for another year, migrating birds fly overhead, and the Virginia creeper twines red in the marina. August is filled with contradictions.

September

September is your month for reflection. After all, you've survived another summer at sea, been baptized "the naviguesser" by the captain, learned a little, and prayed a lot. For example:

- When you're looking out the second floor window of the Baltimore Aquarium and see your boat floating away, you'd better skip the third floor.
- *Mischief* will straighten up when you take everything out of the lazarette, but you won't. Your stomach is permapleated.
- A dinghy full of water and sinking fast makes an unexpected sea anchor. Usually this occurs when dangerous thunderstorms are coming your way and NOAA has issued a Mariners' Alert to take cover as quickly as possible.
- The captain will spend more time trying to rescue the boathook than you when you both fall in the water at the same time. But take heart. ChapWoman has noticed that other captains are more solicitous of your misadventures than your own. When you were floundering about in the water, it was Bill and Harry who rushed to your rescue. You distinctly heard the skipper say,

  "Thanks guys, but I can get the hook."

  "What about your wife?" said Harry.

  "Oh is she in there too?" asked Queeg with more than a little surprise.
- CNG isn't all it's cracked up to be. Now there's a switch for you. All winter you campaigned for it long and hard. No more peering into a puddle of alcohol; just light the gas and presto!—you have a real stove. There's even a temperature control on the oven. The captain, who does not cook, bought an autopilot instead. So . . . Shirley bakes muffins, Helen does roasts, and you still boil in a bag. But boats that smell of muffins and roasts are boats with the mate working below. While you shower in 90-degree heat and zip off

to an air-conditioned restaurant for dinner, Shirley and Helen are wiping the sweat from their brows and slaving in their galleys with only a toy fan for comfort.

"No need to eat out now that we have CNG," chortle their captains, who are topside, of course.

• Fishing is better forgotten. Others may troll for blues, bungie rods to grabrails below, and buy enough surgical tubing for 13 weeks on *General Hospital*. Not you. Oh yes, your captain tried it. He made like an awesome angler demanding his Tony Aceta, but he trolled for a month with Tony and tubing and the only thing he caught was Ezra Goldberg's son's ear. On the eve of his Bar Mitzvah, too. There was young Goldberg, rowing about in his dinghy, and there was your captain taking one last cast. You couldn't blame the kid for shrieking, but you do wish 17 dinghies hadn't raced to the rescue.

• This is your last summer without roller furling. No more hanking on and off for you. You made your pronouncement on one of those typical summer weekends on the bay when NOAA reports 15-to-20 knot winds. NOAA neglects to mention that those winds are gusting up to 80. "Get that genny down in a hurry," barks the captain. You drop the genny on the foredeck at the same moment one of those gusts lifts it. You'd never planned to lay down your life for your genny but instinctively you fling yourself spread-eagled over it and hang on for dear life to the bow pulpit. Your glasses come off their safety strap. One lens pops out. Now you are blind. But that's not all. You are also drowning. Each time *Mischief's* bow goes underwater you go with her. In seconds you have plummeted from the self-actualization bit of Maslow's hierarchy to basic survival. You lie on the foredeck, one hand on the pulpit, one on your lens, blind as a bat, gulping air as *Mischief* scales the crest. You keep your mouth shut when her foredeck vanishes into the trough. And then in the midst of your interminable fight for survival as your life flashes in front of you, you hear your captain's voice,

"What's taking you so long up there?"

You insist that what happened next was an accident. By evening the wind's fury has abated—but your own hasn't. You speak in monosyllables as you approach

You do exactly as he says. Exactly.

the yacht club, where your cruise has reservations for dinner ashore. Your captain wants to shave.

"Just follow that boat in," he says, pointing to the powerboat in front of you. You do exactly as he says. Exactly. The powerboat draws one and a half feet and *Mischief* draws four. One minute you are zipping right along; the next the powerboat continues to zip while *Mischief* lurches to a halt, then lurches again in the opposite direction. The captain bounds onto the deck covered with shaving cream. Blood is coursing down his chin. He grabs the helm and throws it hard over. You suggest that perhaps he would like to wipe his face. He ignores you. In a few minutes *Mischief* is afloat again, but he arrives at the yacht club still coated in shaving cream and blood. Strangers stare, children point, and the dockmaster gives you a slip at the far end of the pier.

• September is the month the kids go back to school. You, too, are back at school. The captain has decreed that the mate must sharpen her sailing skills with the Power Squadron's Advanced Piloting course. Certainly you've already come a long way since you announced your position by saying you were opposite a piece of land that looked like a tennis shoe. Now you can tell the Coast Guard your location, the state of the sea, description of your boat, and the nature of your distress. Part of your distress is having to do all this talking while your boat is sinking.

The captain tells you that AP is more than a course; it is a rite of passage. And if that doesn't clinch it, he reminds you that last summer on your cruise to Williamsburg you ran into an island in the fog because you were 20 degrees off course. Do the same thing with Bermuda and you'll sail on for eternity, he says.

It isn't until a week later, when you are sitting in class with seven engineers, that you remember why you hit the island. The compass had an acute case of the DT's because the captain put the horn in the drink holder. But it's too late to change your mind. Pete, the fleet captain who is teaching the course, is already deep into 60 D street, course over ground, speed and track, and set and drift. You are already confused.

"Well, you're all engineers so you won't have any trouble with the math," says Pete. You are not an engineer. Perhaps you are invisible. Then he acknowledges you with a brief nod.

"Girls can't do math." That does it. You haven't done a parallelogram in 30 years, but right then and there you decide to show them who can do math.

The engineers hang out at break swapping sea stories. Russell picks up his charts and says class is a waste of time; he'll be back to take the exam. You sit alone in the corner practicing the proper way to hold a divider—inside leg with thumb and ring finger, outside leg between first and middle. You've noticed you were the only one in the class using two hands.

The captain gives you a crash course in trig to understand those SOG_1's, SOG_2's that equal S+ current and S- current. Your 1210 training chart is starting to look like a "connect the dots" puzzle. In the dark of night you labor over slack water before flood current and the time of p.m. slack water before ebb at Montauk Point, Alki Point, Puget Sound and Texas Point, Sabine Pass.

Now instead of taking a Judith Krantz novel to bed with you, you take relative bearings of Point Judith light. You tell a startled nonboater at a cocktail party that "True Virgins Make

Dull Company." Finally you complete your cruise and arrive at Nonamettal Island only to discover that one of the engineers has quit, Russell flunks the exam, and you get the highest grade in the class. Who says girls can't do math?

October

Orderly flights of Canada geese pass overhead, the leaves have turned red and gold, and there's a nip in the air.

October has always been *Mischief's* month. Bright clear days with 15 knots of wind and a 20-degree angle of heel are the conditions she loves best. You gunkhole to all your favorite anchorages, sun on her decks, dive from the doghouse, and charcoal off the rail. Closehauled, broad reaching or wing-and-wing, *Mischief* outshines herself. Since it's too late in the season to anchor out, you plug in your heater at dockside and eat dinner below by candlelight. *Mischief's* teak glows warmly in the flickering flame; but you do wish you could redo her upholstery.

"Her orange, brown, and yellow plaid is really out of date," you complain. You'd like to spring for some of that lovely Williamsburg blue velour that all the new boats have. You are not prepared for the captain's next words.

"I don't know if I want to put any more money into *Mischief*. She's 10 years old and past her prime."

Now that you think about it, you have noticed that the gleam in the captain's eye has not been the same.

In April he lusted after Harry's integrated instrument system. And then in the June race series when a 25-foot J-boat left him in the wake, he actually called *Mischief* an "old tub."

"Beam's too narrow, doghouse is too high, and you can't get around the decks in a hurry," he groused.

Back then you chalked it up to sour grapes. After all, he had to blame somebody for the fact that he miscalculated, sailed too wide around the mark, and came in last. But now that you look back on the summer, you realize there were other signs of disillusionment as well. He complained that the port locker always leaked—the same locker he used to affectionately call the goldfish bowl—and that the engine heated the ice chest. You'd been pointing this out to him for years, of course, but it had never made it onto his priority list. "Every boat is a design compromise," he'd say.

Yes, you are caught in a profound loyalty conflict. After all, you, too, look a little different than you did 10 years ago.

Mischief has carried you north and south, soothed you to sleep with lullabies played on her spreaders, stood by you in heavy weather, and picked up a puff with her #180 when everybody else was becalmed. The captain even said he could never love another boat. He said the same thing about you on your honeymoon. You are off on a sentimental roll.

The captain tells you to cool the rhetoric. You can't buy a boat unless you sell *Mischief* and right now the used boat market is soft, but why not start hitting the in-the-water boat shows to at least scope out your next boat? Why not indeed?

So you go the rounds of every show and like kids in a toy store are paralyzed by too many choices. You reject the Taiwanese boats in spite of all the burnished teak skylights and louvres, shelves, rails, and decks. Delivery is one year and you know your captain won't make it through a long dry summer without a boat and you won't make it through a long hot one doing teak.

You do turn on to these high-style French boats with mosaic tile counters below and double beds tucked into every conceivable nook and cranny. Their slim, sleek lines let them slip through the water like torpedoes. Oooo la la! The captain doesn't warm up to them, but you notice with dread that he is making a beeline to the bluewater boats built to be tossed about by a cold and cruel sea. You reject them immediately because you don't want to be put in a position of having to care about great bronze ports designed to hold back the ocean. You avoid the catboat with no ports and a bearded owner who has singlehanded the North Atlantic. Perish the thought. It's better to isolate your captain from that kind of seafarer.

And, of course, there are exquisite boats with prices you can't afford and cheap boats that you might afford but don't want, and racing boats with flat decks and nothing below but 24 bags of sails, and big, cushy, comfortable boats with entertainment centers and bathtubs. They plow through the water like destroyers and are last in every race.

You climb on and off of so many boats that you have permanently shortened your hamstrings. Your captain falls in and out of love every hour, but it's only infatuation. You remain steadfast and loyal. You haven't found another boat like *Mischief*. She's a classy boat if ever there was one, not just some ordinary hussy dressed up to look sharp, or a foreign strumpet with the aura of mystery—exotic woods and far-off lands. You certainly don't want a devil-may-care boat that will introduce you to a life of death and destruction on the high seas.

But you *would* like a beamier boat than *Mischief*, with wider decks and a flatter doghouse so you can see over the top when you are at the helm. An ice chest with a drain in the bottom (instead of an inch above) would be nice, too, and so would Williamsburg blue upholstery.

The questions remain purely academic. You can't afford to buy a boat without selling *Mischief* and nobody wants to buy *Mischief*. So the three of you go right on living together although the captain is definitely dating other boats.

Then suddenly the world turns upside down and you are to blame. It happens by accident, a chance encounter, reminiscent of a 1940s movie, that changes your life forever. The captain is buying antifreeze for *Mischief* in the marine store and talking to Bill about piping into the marina's water supply. You don't want to listen. It means ripping the boat apart again. So you wander about the yard. There in the back is a brand new boat with a ladder propped up against her, no name on the transom, and a "for sale" sign dangling from the rail.

"Why not?" you say to yourself. She's the same make as *Mischief* but eleven years younger—familiar, yet exciting and new at the same time. With a broader beam, wider decks, and a flatter doghouse.

She is solid but still stylish, sleek but comfortable, seaworthy but without a cutter rig and clubfooted jib to knock you out then sweep you into the water. She has enough teak to glow in the candlelight below and teak grabrails, eyebrows, drink holder, and rails above. Her decks are made of fiberglass. She looks like a boat, not a torpedo. There are more drawers below for stowing, a bigger ice chest, two sinks instead of one, refrigeration, CNG—and yes, soft blue upholstery.

Almost in spite of yourself you take the helm and imagine you are sailing the 1210 training chart from Cuttyhunk light to Mishaum Ledge lighted gong buoy and on toward the Dumpling Rocks light.

After looking all around for you, the captain locates you at the helm. At first he thinks you are sick because you are not in the habit of sailing boats in parking lots. Then he thinks

I had a date with a yawl . . .

you are delirious when you explain that this is "your" boat. The world shifts a little when he discovers the integrated instrument system that can obtain vector summation of boat speed and wind speed and arrive at true wind speed and direction. ChapWoman has noticed that electronics are to a man what blue upholstery is to a woman.

"Why not?" he says.

"Why not?" you say. And the next thing you know, you are passing papers, trading *Mischief* in and painting *Why Not* on the transom.

Mischief makes out okay, too. The broker calls you to say that she has been bought by a young couple just learning to sail. He says that of the two, the woman seems to know more than the man.

"It's hard to take her seriously, though, with a name like Kitten," the broker chuckles.

ovember

"We may find that a new boat is an economy," says the captain, shaking hands with the broker and the solemn man from the mortgage company. They smile patiently. Let him keep his delusions for awhile.

They know that the cost of a pipe here and a filter there for *Mischief* is nothing compared with all that *Why Not* needs. She has come into your life wearing only the suit of sails on her back.

Her trousseau will require an anchor, a VHF, a dodger, a bimini, and a stereo. The captain will be working until he's 90 to pay her bills.

"Well, at least we don't have to outfit her until spring," you say hopefully.

"Spring nothing!" explodes the captain—"this year we're going to be November sailors!"

That's the last thing you want to hear. Nobody but a working waterman goes out in November. *Mischief* was always tucked away for her long winter's nap by October 15. Sensing troubled waters ahead, the jovial broker suggests a glass of sherry to toast the occasion. He hands you a book of canvas swatches. Just for today you decide to concentrate on canvas, not conscience.

Good days and bad nights take on a whole new meaning in November. Your first overnight on *Why Not* is honeymoon time. Bursts of red and gold foliage flame on shore, blazing into a brilliant cloudless blue sky. The air is crystal clear, the breeze fresh, the visibility unlimited. Already you feel rapport with liveaboards and are willing to sail on forever wherever the wind blows. This may not be so bad.

In fact, you wonder why nobody else has discovered this magic month of November on the bay. Anchorages that looked like center city parking lots in June are empty. You and the captain sit on deck in the late afternoon sunshine, drinking a toast to *Why Not* and your long life together. You also toast the captain's long life in the workplace. Sunlight dapples the trees and sparkles the water. This is as close to heaven as you are going to get.

When you awake the next morning you have one foot in hell. The cabin that was so cozy when you crawled into your sleeping bag is now damp, clammy, and cold. Rain beats down on the doghouse—not the warm rain of summer but a stinging cold rain that chills the bones and makes the body beg for a hot shower. But who wants to get wet when you can see your breath in the head?

You hear the blast of a shotgun on shore. Armed men are killing ducks. This is definitely a hostile environment.

So you lumber out of bed still encased in your sleeping bag, hop to the galley, and huddle over the steam from the tea kettle. Last night's heavy dew has left a thin coating of ice on the deck. Your bathing suit hanging on the hook is a rebuke.

You power home for four hours in the pouring rain. It didn't matter that your foulweather gear leaked in the summer, but now you suffer loudly as water sneaks in at the collar and trickles down your spine in icy rivulets. ChapWoman has noticed that the captain's foulweather gear never leaks. He is humming.

Certainly, the only sensible thing to do when you reach your slip is to go home. But no, the captain assures you that all will be well and misery a memory as soon as he plugs in the heater. And he might be right if you were into astral traveling or out-of-body experiences that would allow you to float about the cabintop along with the hot air. Instead, your cold lump of a bottom is hopelessly frozen to the settee.

So you are not in a jolly mood when the captain announces that you will be joining a frostbite cruise the following week. The name alone is reason to stay home. But this time you know the score and dress for the occasion in layers of underwear, sweaters, and a ski mask. You look like you're going to hold up a liquor store.

Naturally, you will be on the helm while the captain sits at the chart table with his new integrated instrument system. He can keep track of the true wind speed and direction, the elapsed time, distance, speed, and velocity made good to weather—and you—without ever coming on deck.

He looks like a computer whiz punching all those buttons and bellowing instructions over the gale. He is also drinking hot soup.

The north wind whistles by your ears. *Why Not* picks up speed and suddenly is hit by an unexpected gust. She heels

A frostbite cruise may be judged cruel and unusual punishment and reasonable grounds for divorce.

perilously close to the water. Your scream freezes in your throat but your face is contorted in such a horrible expression that even the captain is alarmed. He bounds up on deck, shortens sail, and pats you on the back.

"No need to worry, the water is warmer than the air today." In case he hadn't noticed, you mention that you are not a storm petrel and you want to go home. Not overboard. At moments like this it is easy to understand why frostbite cruising is considered cruel and unusual punishment and reasonable grounds for divorce.

November wears on. The marina empties and the parking lot fills with boats, not cars. You are still there, spending money at the marine store. They keep it open on Saturdays just for you. The cruisers heading down the ICW to Florida left in October. Helen and Shirley have abandoned you. They glare at the captain, offer you their pity and go home to snug houses in New Jersey to listen to the weather on television rather than be out in it. Even the crabs have gone south.

A few old salts are left. They talk about boating accidents, accidental drownings, and underwear. Although you can

The boat and the mate are riding high. The car and the captain have hit bottom. Boating season is over.

debate in depth the merits of thermolactic or polypro, you are quite aware that you are turning into a boring conversationalist.

They shut off the water in the marina. You are still there.

"Let's make it to Thanksgiving. We could have dinner aboard," says the captain.

You gulp. Thanksgiving has never been an easy time, but on a boat . . . . Come to think of it, though, it might not be such a bad idea. At home you cook turkey for 22 relatives including the captain's second cousin whom you can't stand and his wife who always complains about the sweet potato casserole. On the boat it will be just Ralph and Susie and Howlyard.

You are amazed that the kids agree to your great escape. The weather cooperates with your romanticism. Thanksgiving day dawns clear, bright, and 60 degrees. The turkey is in the oven at eight o'clock and you are off for a glorious sail. The leaves are gone from the trees, but the air is warm. You are stripped down to a sweater and Ralph to his stomach. Howlyard snoozes in a sunny spot on the cabin sole. The aroma of turkey wafts up on the deck. No football or parades, telephone, or TV. Just you, your family, the sun, and the wind. Who could ask for more?

At two o'clock you sit down for turkey, mashed potatoes, gravy, and all the trimmings. Aside from the fact that you can't go to the head without folding up the table and dumping dinner in everybody's lap, you look like any family celebrating Thanksgiving, only yours is better. But it is a bittersweet weekend as well because this is the last sail of the season.

When you return a week later, *Why Not* is up on blocks and it is snowing. You are grim and miserable as you make wheelbarrow trip after wheelbarrow trip to the car. The captain strips her of her batteries and fills her tank with antifreeze that looks like the red tide. Finally he wraps her in a great blue shroud.

With fingers stiff, freezing, and clumsy in gloves, you struggle to help tie the strings. The wet snow sticks to your jacket and hood and stings your face. This is torture. Finally *Why Not* is entombed for the winter. Only a spelunker would enter her now.

You push the last wheelbarrow load to the car and notice that while you and *Why Not* are riding high, the captain and car are very low. Boating season is over.

ecember

You have never been able to look a gift horse in the mouth, so when the captain suggests lunch and a Christmas shopping spree you jump at the invitation.

There you are sipping a glass of wine and dreaming of the elegant coat in Bloomingdale's window when the captain takes your hand. He is humming.

"How would you like a plow for Christmas?" he asks. To gild the lily he adds fifty feet of chain so you will never drag again. You may never leave the anchorage again, either.

To be frank, a plow had not been at the top of your list or even the bottom. But *Why Not* does need an anchor because the one you were using was borrowed. So you agree that this year, *Why Not* will be the kid at Christmas. The first stop on the shopping spree will be the marine store.

The marine store looks like Christmas in the islands, with Santa sitting in a rubber dinghy. Holly and red ribbon twine around the lifesling, and a huge wreath hangs over the hardware department. Eager elves in bright red aprons help enthusiastic skippers spend big bucks on their boats.

You run into your old marina mate, Bill, in the electronics department. He is ogling a Loran. He wants it. In fact it is obvious to everybody including the salesman that he has never wanted any piece of equipment so much in his life. He wonders if Marge will understand. At times like this mates stick together.

"Absolutely not," you say. Of course it might be different if he gave her CNG. Bill perks up and you know a deal is in the making.

For a while you wander aimlessly behind the captain admiring snatch blocks, shackles, and davits, but soon the hardware begins to pall. The cosmetic counter at Bloomies it definitely is not.

So you break apart and discover an aisle filled with dishes, cutlery, and placemats. This is more like it. *Mischief* came into your life used and was outfitted with hand-me-downs—the leftover Melmac from home and unmatched stainless—but *Why Not* deserves the finer things in life.

Getting into the Christmas spirit, you merrily outfit the galley with dishes and glasses decorated with flags, matching cutlery, and designer trash bags. Moving right along, you spot the monogrammed cocktail napkins right across the aisle from the monogrammed sweaters. You had monogrammed sheets in your trousseau, so why shouldn't *Why Not* have monogrammed napkins in hers? You toss a sweater into your basket for good measure.

You are having such a good time that you forget you are even in a marine store until you hear the captain's voice. His basket is filled with your gifts: a plow, handfuls of hardware, polypropylene line, a new white horseshoe, and a teak magazine rack.

"What is the mate doing?" he asks, eyeing your basket full of goodies.

"Buying your Christmas presents," you say sweetly.

On Christmas Eve you put the last gift under the twinkling tree and smile at all the packages wrapped in nautical paper and, of course, the plow. It has a bright red ribbon around it and a card saying, "To the Mate With Love." It's going to be the best Christmas ever, even though it is *Why Not* who has made out like a bandit. Of course, Ralph and Susie think you are a little nutty, but that's nothing new.

When you open *their* gifts the next morning you discover matching blue T-shirts saying, "The Captain" and "The Navigator." Navigator, not mate! You stand a little taller after that. The captain starts counting days on his new nautical calendar.

"Commissioning is only 67 days away," he says.

Later that day the relatives start arriving for Christmas dinner and the captain settles down to read "The Night Before Christmas" to his nieces and nephews. This year it has a new twist:

> T'was the night before Christmas when all through
> the slip,
> Not a halyard was singing on our little ship.
> The stockings were hung from the mizzen with care,
> In hopes that Saint Nicholas soon would be there.
> The children were nestled all snug, one per bunk,
> Tuned in to their rock groups and also to punk.

And the mate in her longjohns and I in my shorts,
Had just settled down from a round of rum snorts,
When up above decks there arose such a clatter,
I sprang from my berth to see what was the matter.
Away in a twinkling I flew to the hatch,
Jumped over my leeboard and threw up the latch.
The moon hanging bright at the top of the rigging,
Gave a luster of midday that was quite intriguing.
When what to my wondering eyes should appear,
But a miniature sloop and eight tiny reindeer!
With a little old sailor so lively and quick,
I knew in a moment it must be Saint Nick.
More rapid than speedboats his coursers they came,
And he whistled and shouted and called them by
    name.
"Now Spanker, now Clinker, now Painter and
    Boomkin,
On Scupper, on Drifter, on Camber and Bumkin."
To the top of the mast, then down to the spreader,
They were getting so close I could see them much
    better.
As small craft that before a wild thunderstorm flee,
When the squall finally hits, seek the calm of a lee,
So onto the foredeck his coursers they flew,
With the aid of Loran and a depth-finder, too.
In less than a twinkling, on deck I could hear,
The pawing and prancing of each little deer.
As I drew in my head and gulped hard for the teak,
Down the hatchway Saint Nicholas came for a peek.
He was dressed all in oilskins from his head to his toe,
And they glistened with salt spray—a bright yellow
    glow.
A large duffel of gifts he carried with ease,
And he looked like a mariner home from the seas.
His eyes how they squinted, his eyebrows how
    craggy,
His cheeks were windburned, his beard slightly
    shaggy.
His droll little mouth was drawn up in a grin,

And his smile was as bright as a new Halogen.
A safety line held him on fairly close tether,
(I guess sailing at Christmas, you encounter rough
   weather.)
He had a broad beam and right portly girth,
Like a spinnaker drawing for all that it's worth.
He was chubby and plump, a right jolly old salt,
And I laughed when I saw him, but that's not my
   fault.
The way he said "Aye Aye" after using the head,
Soon gave me to know I had nothing to dread.
He set to his work (there was plenty to do),
And filled all the stockings—the water tanks, too.
Then laying a finger port side of his nose,
And giving a nod, through the hatchway he rose.
He sprang to his vessel, to his crew gave command,
And at once cast off, with myself as dockhand.
But I heard him exclaim as he tacked out of sight,
"Ahoy to all this Christmas!
Bon voyage and good night!"

The Captain's Horoscope

Capricorn
(December 22-January 20)

The Capricorn captain is not a party animal. No, he does not believe in play. Let others test their wits at Trivial Pursuit and the sailor's game. He's down in the dinghy compounding the hull. For recreation he oils teak or reads *The 12-Volt Doctor's Alternator Book*.

He is calm, deliberate, and knowledgeable. There is no careless abandon aboard his vessel. He gives a brief lesson on sailing "by the woolies" before he releases the helm. Pinching has only one meaning topside—to windward. While his cruising mates stay rafted up for one more drink, he breaks apart and motors alone to a protected anchorage. He is sitting cozily under his dodger watching the fray when their anchors drag, thunder roars, and lightning streaks the sky.

Capricorn runs a taut ship: no idle chatter topside or catching the rays with a book. On his vessel it's every man on a winch and tie the lines with sutures. He learns to resilver his sextant mirrors because you never know when you might need to know that sort of thing at sea. Even Bowditch recommends having it done professionally.

Capricorn wants a return on his investment so he puts his boat up for charter. Let other captains turn their $100,000 toys over to charter companies—Capricorn does it himself. He is there checking references, greeting at the marina, and waiting on the dock when the boat returns. Sure, he makes the charterers nervous, but there is no damage aboard his boat.

He respects tradition. His ensign is raised exactly two-thirds of the way up the backstay, no more, no less, at exactly 0800 hours, not a second sooner or later. He cares about his colors. On regatta days his vessel is dressed to the nines right down to canvas covers on each winch. He enjoys saluting. He would rather drown than dirty his horseshoe.

He rarely deviates to right or left. Expect him to fall into your boat when the dock turns and he goes straight. It is prudent for the mate to take the helm when the crab pots bob ahead or freighters loom on the horizon.

CAPRICORN—Sitting on deck with an air rifle.

He is persistent. The mate must put everything in its proper place although you may notice that he puts nothing in its place. He never gives up when swallows swoop above the deck. He starts with a black rubber hose on deck, moves on to the kids' green plastic snake, followed by an owl, and finally winds up sitting on deck with an air rifle.

He never panics, so party poop or not, he is your captain of choice when you lose steerageway in a shipping lane or discover the cabin lights were on all day and are dead.

quarius
(January 21-February 19)

The Aquarius captain may have his head in the stars with Bowditch and his hand on the tiller with Columbus, but he's cool, calm, and collected in a knockdown.

He's both a realist and a future thinker who plans his great escape to Moorea and Tahiti long before he can afford to. He sells his sleek, swift 28-footer and buys a 37-foot bluewater boat with a six-foot fixed keel. It backs like an elephant. Sure, he may spend as much time aground in the bay as afloat, but he's advancing toward his dream.

Let others sit by the fire in January. He's down at the marina in earmuffs and nose warmer shoveling the snow off the decks and planning an early commissioning. He goes out with the ice breakers.

Aquarius is rarely where you expect him to be because he ignores his sailing itinerary and goes where the wind blows. You won't find him beating to Block if he can sail on a broad reach to Cuttyhunk—in spite of the fact that his friends were meeting him for lobsters at Baxter's on Block.

He saves everything the mate wants to throw out. His ditty bag bulges with bits of Velcro, odd lengths of lines, bolts and screws, and small wedges of teak. These mere scraps of booty might be just what he needs sometime. When he installed a hawse hole and a hatch he put the sawed-off pieces of fiberglass in the attic. The mate has moved them from Massachusetts to Maryland because she doesn't dare throw them out.

While others sleep below, Aquarius is up on deck 'til dawn gazing at the twinkling anchor lights and darkened hulls swaying sweetly in the breeze. And if a light goes on in the porthole of the 60-foot cabin cruiser across the way, expect him to do a bit of rubbernecking with the binoculars.

Count on Aquarius to handle the insane or unstable. When fearful Aunt Florence's fingers lock for eternity around a winch, it is soothing Aquarius who pries her loose.

He is calm and reassuring when his vessel hits an underwater obstruction and starts filling up with water. The quieter he

AQUARIUS—He goes out with the ice breakers.

gets, the more life-threatening the situation. When he whispers it's time to swim for it.

He's your captain of choice when your boat starts climbing the floating docks in Baltimore Harbor because the throttle lever has jammed. Sure, he leaves the mate alone on deck while he goes below to get a screwdriver, but once back he fixes the problem and soothes the mate's hysterics at the same time.

isces
(February 20-March 20)

The Pisces captain is a laid-back mariner. He's not into power or leadership. Let someone else be commodore, fleet captain, or flag lieutenant. No afterguard or uniforms for him. You'll find him in torn jeans, cooking 200 hamburgers for the annual sail club beach party. Breakfasts on his boat are the best afloat.

He's a dreamer—Huck Finn in docksiders sailing down-wind with his course punched into the autohelm. Perhaps he'll retire, sell the house and the cars, and live aboard. Perhaps he'll winter in the islands. He's just as likely to wind up in the South China Sea.

Pisces is careless about tomorrow. His is not a shipshape boat. His teak may be blackened from neglect and his lines are thrown below, not carefully stowed in proper places. His lockers and lazarette are a Virgo nightmare and his tool drawer a jumble. Forget fitting the screwdrivers into matching cutouts. But in spite of the confusion, Pisces knows what counts. His lines are in perfect working order and there's never a bag in his sails.

He rarely plans ahead. That's him arriving for race week with his seabag packed and no crew assignment. He hangs out at the dock. The next time you see him, he's hoisting the racing spinnaker of a 42-foot sloop. The one that wins.

He doesn't like to swim upstream. He'd rather sail like hell off the wind and with the current than tack back and forth across the bay. He'll drive to a rendezvous instead of beating to windward. He prefers dinner ashore to cleaning the charcoal grill.

When Pisces thinks something bad is going to happen it usually does, so listen up when he cancels the Bermuda trip a week before the race. Sure, you're in your berth in Marion dreaming about the Princess Hotel. What you don't know is that one boat will sink and three will be dismasted before the party at the Princess.

He's a practical joker. There's only a mast showing in the water where your boat should be. It's coronary time. The

PISCES—Cooking 200 hamburgers.

insurance binder has not arrived. No, your vessel has not sunk, although Pisces would like you to think so. He's moved it to another slip.

Pisces' first instinct is to help. He's your captain of choice when you buy a new boat because he offers to work with you to get ready for launch. And later when your engine fails with the current carrying you to certain destruction on a bridge abutment, it is Pisces who answers your "Pan Pan."

ries
(March 21-April 20)

Aries would rather be caught dead than weak. You'll find him out on the foredeck hanking on the jib in 20-knot winds with the waves washing over him. None of this namby-pamby roller furling for him. The only time he wears a safety harness is when the depth-finder registers 100 fathoms.

He goes sailing for fun on days when the men who make their living on the sea stay home. Small craft warnings are his aphrodisiac. He hoists his sails at 5:00 a.m. and averages 70 miles a day.

He drives himself and his boat to the limit. He's nonchalant about knockdowns. It's no wonder that all his stanchions and chainplates leak.

Nobody can do anything as efficiently as Aries. That's what he thinks. He unties and reties all the lines, unlocks and relocks the lockers, and would like to be at the helm and the anchor at the same time. No, he does not share command. His is not an equal-opportunity vessel. He knows more about the engine than the marina does. It's better not to ask him why there is a clothespin separating two engine wires.

He is never wrong. He decides that the other boat dragged anchor last night—the one he has just run into. Who cares if the vessel in question would have had to move forward 30 feet against the current? And no, the freighter on the horizon is anchored in spite of the fact that the mate sees a wisp of smoke in the stacks. He does not order a course change until he sees the whites of the other captain's eyes. Then he chastises the mate for being on a collision course.

Aries leads all marches. He never follows. When the rest of the cruise veers off to starboard in a new anchorage, Aries charges ahead under full sail alone, and is soon hard aground.

The mate suggests pegs in the lazarette and a light in the galley. He vetoes the idea. Later he suggests pegs for the lazarette and a light in the galley. There is no victory with Aries, only peaceful coexistence.

ARIES—When the baby falls overboard, it is only Aries who can scoop him up in a crab net and make the 12 o'clock bridge opening.

But he is without equal in a crisis. Aries is your captain of choice when the sails rip and the tiller splits in weather you shouldn't be out in. And when the baby falls overboard, it is only Aries who can scoop him up in a crab net and still make the 12 o'clock bridge opening.

♉ aurus
(April 21-May 21)

Taurus is stubborn and bullheaded. He is never off course; it is the Baltimore light that has moved. Once he has made up his mind he will not change. "I'll Do It My Way" was written for him.

Expect him to stick to his goals long after others have given up. Particularly when it comes to the cruise itinerary. He honors his destination above all else. Sure, there are gale warnings but determined Taurus will tough it out in the rain at a 40 degree angle of heel to reach the specified anchorage. Of course he'll be alone when he gets there. The rest of the cruise is having a blast in Annapolis. Taurus never stays home on a summer weekend. You can also look forward to bobbing and sweating in 100 degree heat.

It's no surprise that his family suffers from early burnout. The rite of passage celebration at his house is graduation from Dad's crew. His children rarely return to the water.

Look out when Taurus charts a course for the boat show. He'll ask the mate's opinion on buying a spinnaker, a dodger, an autopilot, or a new boat because he'd like you to agree. So agree. He's going to buy it anyway.

He is a practical problem solver and planner instead of a worrier. He carries in his wallet a computer printout of every locker, with all the contents neatly labeled. On his boat, there's no wondering where the Dinty Moore, flares, or two child-size life jackets are stowed. He can find them when he's still at home.

When he lies in bed staring blankly at the ceiling, he is either tracing the water leak to the port locker or mentally ripping out half the mate's galley to replace the old Atomic 4 with a new diesel.

Catch him staring out to sea and it probably means that the gas tank is empty. He is figuring out how to tack into the slip with the wind on the nose. Little disturbs his tranquility.

He's into male camaraderie and macho shorthanded sailing to Bermuda. Sure, he's seasick steadily for four days, but

TAURUS—It is the Baltimore light that has moved.

when the vessel passes the Bermuda light, he's the first to open the Mount Gay Rum.

There are lots of times when you'd rather not sail with him, but romantic Taurus is your captain of choice when the full moon rises over the bay. Cassiopeia, Polaris, and Ursa Major never looked so good. Yes, Taurus tosses lines to the mates and handles more than the winches.

emini
(May 22-June 21)

The Gemini captain does two things at once with less effort than it takes the mate to hold a compass course. That's him at the helm checking the charts with his right hand and tuning the sails with his left, coaxing an extra knot of speed out of his vessel while adjusting his heading to compensate for set and drift.

Gemini is into changing plans. The mate intends dinner ashore for her guests. Gemini sets his course for a protected anchorage where shy long-legged herons stand at the water's edge. It's a lovely spot if only he'd mentioned it sooner. The nearest restaurant is 50 miles as the crow flies. It's either fish or starve.

He considers changing course to check a buoy number a sign of weakness. Perish the thought. He looks at the scenery, he looks at the chart, and he "knows" exactly where he is. The mate is not so sure. She suggests that one piece of bay scenery looks pretty much like another unless it's the Calvert Cliffs. Why not come about to check the nun at the mouth of the river? "Out of my way—Never," says Bligh. It's a lot more out of his way when he discovers that he is one hour up the right fork of the river and the boat with the dinner is anchored in the left fork.

He's a promoter and a charming intellect. He brings a few customers sailing—and his neighbor with whom he brews beer in the basement—and writes the boat off as a business expense. He throws in the slip fee and the mileage for good measure. The used boat market is never soft for him. Sure, his boat leaks from every stanchion and chainplate and there's snow on the decks, but Gemini has the heater running two hours before his customer arrives. There's wine and cheese on the table and an oil lamp casting a cozy glow. Who cares about the delamination topside? Boating never looked so good.

Gemini is your captain of choice whenever you play Nautical Pursuits. You can count on him to know the name of the

GEMINI—It's either fish or starve.

only seven-masted schooner ever built, where to find a "blind buckler" and the year Vasco de Gama made his first voyage to India. What's a little indecision compared with that?

ancer
(June 22-July 23)

The Cancer captain is pessimistic. He has a vague sense of nameless dangers lurking out there in the briny deep. For every porpoise frolicking beside his vessel he imagines a whale about to flip him down to Davy Jones' locker. His will be the craft that vanishes in the Bermuda Triangle.

Yes, he's into doom and gloom. He suffers a lot and dreams of sinking. He tops off the gas tank and the water tank for a one-hour sail, and on a weekend he carries enough provisions for two weeks at sea, because you never know what might happen. He worries about what might come out of the heavens. He's sure that it is going to rain, that you'll never get where you are going under sail, and of course you will run aground. He sets anchor half a mile from the nearest boat because someone, somewhere, will either swing or drag.

Yet in spite of all his pessimism he is drawn to the water. He hangs out at marinas and waterfronts and gets his midweek fix on the Staten Island ferry.

He's a traditionalist at heart. He'd really prefer canvas over Mylar and Kevlar, but settles for simple Dacron sails. He considers a fully battened main suspect. He sails a 1960 Pearson because boats were built better back then, he says, with a higher quality of glass. Perhaps, but they were ugly as sin below with no hull liners and all the nasty side of the fiberglass showing. Yes, his ship is dark and dreary below with a galley that would shame Columbus. He's a Tall Ships groupie who is into baggywrinkle. His idea of a vacation is four days on the ocean on the *Mystic Clipper*.

Cancer never gives up the old things he likes—not his torn college sweatshirt, his 10-year-old boat shoes or, of course, his boat. His 1960 Pearson is barely broken in. He goes to the boat show every year, checks out all the vessels, and decides that this is not the year to step up. The new-fangled boats with wider beams, entertainment centers, double sinks, CNG, microwaves, and vee-berths designed for humans with feet, not mermaids, don't turn him on. He'd rather sell the

CANCER—For every frolicking porpoise he imagines a whale.

house than his old Pearson.

The Cancer captain likes to have his family around him. His is the boat with kids clinging to the doghouse and dangling from the bowsprit. Even the dog takes its place at the helm.

The mate may complain that the Cancer captain moves sideways instead of in the direction of what he wants, but it's just this habit that makes him your captain of choice when somebody falls overboard. He may not rise instantly to the crisis like an Aries, but at least he won't plow into the passenger floundering about in the water.

eo
(July 24-August 23)

The Leo captain is an extrovert. He's into dramatic action and being the center of attention. No slipping quietly into an anchorage for him. He sails in with spinnaker, staysail, and five sails flying, oblivious to the terror of the captains and their mates. They stand on deck in life jackets, ready to fend off disaster or abandon ship if disaster strikes. Once he finds the perfect spot, he shouts, "Drop sails, drop the hook!" and everything goes down at once. He spins to a stop. He never motors to his mooring. Expect to find him out flying a spinnaker with the Naval Academy racing team in 20-knot winds. All the other boats are reefed.

He's a daring offshore sailor, always straining for the outward edge, but never solo. Leo commands his crew and delegates the messy jobs to mates and grinders. That's what they are for. Back in inland waters you won't find him cleaning the scum out of the bilge, the slime from the ice chest, the oozing grey anchor mud from the bow, or the sea nettle out of the shower sump; the mate will. He does not clean his own fish.

He's full of vitality. His sailing season never ends. He sails in bright October weather; he sails in chill, dreary November; he sails in crisp, cold December with a holly wreath hanging from the spreader. The kids and the mate quit in October, the dog and his friend who served duty on an icebreaker quit in November, but Leo insists that there are a few warm days in December. And then there is the February thaw.

He's a super organizer and anybody's pick for cruise chairman. Only Leo can sandwich 18 boats into a sunflower raft undamaged, particularly when one comes in bow first with the throttle stuck on high. No sooner is the last boat trussed than Leo is down in the dinghy in a sombrero serving margaritas. And when it's time for the cruise dinner, he remembers who ordered chicken, or fish, and who forgot to pay.

He's an expert on all things nautical. Check with him before you buy roller furling, a diesel, refrigeration, or a cabin

LEO—He complains about his filet of sole marguerite.

heater, but then you'd better take his advice. When he tells you where to go for the best seafood in Nantucket and you say you want fancy French cuisine, he'll sulk for the rest of the evening—and complain about his filet of sole marguerite.

Leo prefers to be leaned on than to lean, so he is your captain of choice when you think you are going to die at sea. There you are scaling waves that put the Death Ride at the state fair to shame and sliding down their trough to your certain end when Leo puts his arm around you and assures you that you will live to see the dawn. And you believe him.

Virgo
(August 24-September 23)

The Virgo captain is a neat, methodical perfectionist. He keeps the Dust-Buster busy below and his lines in perfect working order topside. His winches double as make-up mirrors. Others may stuff their sails and roll up the sail cover in a ball. Not Virgo. All his canvas is folded precisely in neat flat squares. There's always extra room in his sail bag. He spends his spare time training the mainsail to flake over the boom.

He is just as fastidious about his grooming. He dresses with understated nautical elegance—no frayed cutoffs by day or old khakis by night—his shorts have soft leather patches and his shirts are discreetly monogrammed with boat name or yacht club. He's a G.Q. captain if ever there was one. While the rest of the crew is throwing up, you'll find him out in a howling rainstorm with a cake of soap, stark naked except for his safety harness. He's a vision of sartorial splendor when he boards his inflatable.

His liquor locker is full of bottles in proper cutouts. He drinks gin or vodka at the end of the day in tall frosty glasses that he stores in the refrigerator. His is not a beer-in-cans kind of boat.

Anxious Virgo is a worrier who can't relax and be carefree. No dodgeball with freighters for him. He keeps the rules of the road next to his heart and frets about that mere speck on the horizon. Who has the right of way? He mistakes airplanes for storm clouds and times the squall lines with his stopwatch.

He can't sit still. It's trim and tune the sails, move the genny from the inner to the outer track, put up the blooper, adjust the mizzen, loosen the outhaul. After all that he changes his mind, changes his course, and resets all the sails. The instant the crew collapses he decides to hoist the racing spinnaker.

He is precise. When he sets anchor he gives the mate so many hand signals you think he's signaling football plays. He sits on the bow for two tide changes to be sure the anchor doesn't drag.

VIRGO—You'll find him in a howling rainstorm with a cake of soap.

He likes to sail from one spot to another and to know exactly where he is going before he leaves the slip. He's not into cruises to nowhere, aimless tacking, or drifting about at two knots. He uses his binoculars for buoys, not bikinis.

Perhaps he seems a bit antisocial when he chooses to dingy over to the sunflower raft instead of joining the confusion. But dependable Virgo is your captain of choice on the offshore passage to New England. While the rest of the crew sleeps, he holds a compass course for four hours and never gets the wrong star in the spreader.

Libra
(September 24-October 23)

The Libra captain is never careless. His lines are labeled, color-coded, looped, and neatly coiled. They never fray or foul. Libra knows the score. He takes relative bearings on every ship on the horizon, washes the sail at night with a flashlight in the Ambrose shipping channel, and memorizes the COLREGS pecking order for right of way at sea.

Careful he may be, but he isn't orderly. He either loses his possessions or forgets their names. In an emergency he barks at the mate to grab the "whatchamacallit" in a hurry. Sails flap and waves wash over the deck while the mate plays 20 questions. Is the "whatchamacallit" bigger than a bread box? And then he can't find the "whosit" to open the water tanks. The mate turns the boat upside down looking for the "whosit." Then Libra finds the "whosit," which of course is the key, in his pocket.

Like a balance scale, Libra goes up and down. On the upswing he cleans and oils all the teak, compounds the hull, scrubs the barnacles off the dinghy, and polishes the bowsprit and the stanchions. He covets a J-boat with 20 bags of sails in the vee-berth. After each afternoon spin around the bay he has an orgy with deck mop and suds. On the downswing he can't be bothered to get the sails out of their bags, so he motors and talks about trawlers. The teak turns black, the stanchions are pocked with salt spray, and he hangs out in the slip with a cold beer.

Libra dislikes making instant decisions. There's something irrevocable about deciding to drop the hook. He motors about the anchorage until sunset trying to find the perfect spot. And then when the boat settles he is too close to his neighbor, the rode isn't tight enough for his liking or he swings over his neighbor's anchor, so he moves. Again and again.

He's argumentative. If the mate wants to go to Block Island by the inside route he chooses the ocean route; if she wants to go ashore to pick crabs he wants to catch his own; when the mate wants to go home because she hears thunder he stays

LIBRA—Grab the "whatchamacallit."

and says it's just a sonic boom. Then the boat is struck by lightning.

Libra loves his friends and hates crowds of strangers. He won't take you to dinner in Annapolis or Edgartown, but he's your captain of choice for a raft-up in the Great Salt Pond. A bottle of wine and dinner on Libra's boat is about as hospitable as life gets.

89

corpio
(October 24-November 22)

The Scorpio captain is exhilarated by adventure and adversity. Thirty-five knot winds, five-foot seas and the mate riding the boom out over the black inferno gives a fillip to his day. She was taking down the sails when the boat did a 360. Scorpio gets the boat and the mate under control. His eyes sparkle. The mate wants last rites.

When his anchor drags and resets itself in 70-knot hurricane gusts, Scorpio is up on deck in his scivvies in the deluge warding off the daymark to port and the expensive yacht to starboard with all the zip of a spectator at a tennis match.

Scorpio is into winning. He removes the table and the hot water tank for the race season and plots revenge to any captain who forces him to luff up. Of course he's up for stealing any wind he can get. "Mast Abeam" is his pet call.

He strains relationships topside with his explosive temper. He shouts, yells, and barks orders at the deck crew. He takes his sailing seriously—no weakness is allowed aboard his vessel. So what if you think you have broken your arm? Get on that winch and start cranking. He sees his crew as extensions of himself. If he had been born with eight arms he'd always sail alone, because he's a loner at heart, happiest singlehanding.

He is a law unto himself, unconcerned about what others think. He arrives in an anchorage, puts down 300 feet of chain and announces on a megaphone that he may swing. Or, he drops 20 times more rode than he needs and immediately goes out to dinner. The wind shifts and his boat spends the rest of the evening meandering through the anchorage. When he returns he is oblivious to all the captains on deck with flashlights.

Scorpio carries a grudge—years later he will remember the skipper who filed a protest against him at Block Island Race Week—but a friend of Scorpio is a friend for life. When you and your boat are in Cape May and your car is in Annapolis, it is Scorpio who will drive those extra miles to reconnect car and captain.

SCORPIO—His eyes sparkle. The mate wants last rites.

Scorpio meets troubles head on and conquers them, so he is your captain of choice when the engine warning bell rings, the engine stops, and horrible black glop spews out of the exhaust. In seconds he makes like a frogman in goggles and mask and is down under the boat scrubbing nettles off the intake screen.

⚓agittarius
(November 23-December 21)

The Sagittarian captain should call his boat *Tactless*. He's blunt but never malicious, always putting his foot in his mouth. He says he likes your new boat. Then he adds that it doesn't look as cheap as it is. A tricky wind sneaks around the stern. His guest at the helm jibes, "Been sailing long?" says Sagittarius. "All my life," says guest. "You'd never know it," says Sagittarius.

He pushes all hands off the rail into the water when he runs aground. Better for leverage. Like crabs beside the boiling pot, they clutch each other, paralyzed in terror. He neglected to ask if anybody could swim.

Sagittarius is restless. While his crew sleeps he paces from vee-berth to salon to aft cabin to galley to deck. Then he plunks down on the quarter berth and turns on the infrared to study tomorrow's charts. A groan comes from the quarter berth, where he may have broken both legs of the crewmember sleeping there. He turns on all the cabin lights to apologize and wakes up the three other crewmembers and the dog.

He's attracted to danger. You'll find him either dodging bombs in restricted naval areas, weighing anchor in the fog, or sailing right up to the promenade deck of *QE II* before he comes about. He thinks a crisis at sea is running out of gin. Getting dismasted in the Ambrose shipping channel is a mere inconvenience.

Sagittarius is gregarious. No sitting in a corner of the cockpit for him. He's the life of the party who brings all the water balloons to the raft-up and a slingshot as well. Count on him to keep the booze flowing and the raft singing all 42 verses to "If All Little Girls Were Like Fish In The Ocean." His nettle pool is shut down by the marine police.

He drinks beer, wears jeans and an old navy watch cap, and shares the helm with anybody who wants it.

Friendly Sagittarius will never turn away from a call for help, so he is your captain of choice whenever you run

SAGITTARIUS—He neglected to ask if anybody could swim.

aground. He will see you waving your arms, rush to your rescue, toss you a line, and stick with you until you are off.